The Light Dep Growers Guide:
How to Harvest Marijuana Multiple Times a Year

JAMES DEFENBAUGH

Copyright © 2016 James Defenbaugh

All rights reserved.

ISBN: 1530564565
ISBN-13: 978-1530564569

DEDICATION

This book is dedicated to the renegade entrepreneurs who beat to the tune of their own drum and do things differently.

CONTENTS

1	Multiply Your Harvest- Why Light Dep?	1
2	What is Light Dep	8
3	Choosing a Location for Your Structure	11
4	Building Your Own Light Dep Greenhouse	14
5	Choosing the Right Light Dep Tarp	17
6	How to Cover & Uncover Your Manual Dep	22
7	Automatic Light Dep	26
8	Timing of Dep Covering & Uncovering	30
9	When is the Right Time to Begin Depping?	31
10	Lighting	34
11	Strains	39
12	Watering	44
13	Microbes	49
14	Vegetative Growth	55
15	Flowering	59
16	Ventilation	65
17	Soil	68
18	Pots vs. Beds	72
19	Open Air vs. Greenhouse	76
20	Plant Density & Creating a Canopy	80
21	Harvest	85
22	Hiring Help	90
23	Planning Ahead & Problem Solving	92
24	Staging/Time Line/ The Plan	97

1 MULTIPLY YOUR HARVEST- WHY LIGHT DEP?

Multiplying your harvests is the only way to increase your production. All it takes is a first-rate plan and the right set up. The pages of this book will give you exactly that. All you have to do is read and learn. Take some notes and before you know it you will be pulling multiple harvests in one year.

The plan is the most important part of the operation simply because without it you won't know where to start. I have found that the best way to achieve a goal is to visualize that goal and work backwards from there. Huh? First you need to have a goal.

Let's say your goal is to harvest cannabis three times in one year using light dep. What you want to do is figure out when your third harvest will take place. Let's say it will be October 30. Now what we need to do is go backwards in the calendar to figure out when the second harvest should take place. Once we have that figured out it's time to start thinking about when the first harvest should take place. Okay, now we have our harvest dates and all we need to do now is develop a plan to achieve the first, second and third harvest! Sounds simple right? Well it's far more complex than it sounds, but relax. By the time you finish reading this book you will know exactly what to do, how to set up your grow, and how to harvest three times a year using light dep.

Stabilizing and increasing your production stream is the objective of this book. This book is here to make sure that you no longer have to live in the feast and famine cycle. By removing yourself from the feast and famine cycle you will be able to reduce your stress and live better. What are we, hunter gatherers? No we are not! And we shouldn't have to live like they did.

You may be wondering what I'm talking about when I say "feast or famine." Well, it's simple really. In the recent past if you grew outdoors you were stuck with one harvest a year. You had to wait for months before harvesting. And when you did harvest you had tons of work but some good money too. What it also meant was you had to live off of that income for twelve months. You had to pay all your bills, buy food, entertainment, and pay for family expenses from what you made the previous year. If you are like so many others out there (me included) making a budget and sticking to it is not really something you excel at. Subsequently, when the end of the season came around you were probably dead broke and barely getting by.

Well, thank goodness for light dep! With light dep you are able to pull in *at least* two or three harvests a year. Meaning you are able to get paid about half way through the season, around June or July. Say goodbye to being dead broke in October! This makes life so much easier because you now have some money to work with: maybe take a small vacation or just pay the bills. This also reduces the stress of waiting months on end for one harvest because now you have enough money to survive on if for some reason you don't get to harvest a second time.

Scarcity is one of the great benefits of harvesting in the middle of the year. In summer all of last year's outdoor product is gone or soon to be gone. Because this is the case, demand is up and you will have exactly what people want. Not only will you have what they want, but it will be fresh. Your product will be vibrant green and have that full body aroma. You will only have to compete with last year's outdoor which will have lost some smell and definitely lost some of its color. And if last year's wasn't cured and stored right it could even be musty and brown, but that is a story for another time.

The best part though are the prices. Not only are they better than in fall (actually a hell of a lot better!) but you will be able to move it out fast. Not sitting around wondering when someone is going to come along to buy it. What was a hard task in November should be an easy task in July. You basically went from a pest in November to a welcome guest in July! Those days of competition are gone until the return of October when the fall harvest is in and the market is completely saturated.

Anytime you have the opportunity to stabilize your income stream and get better prices you should LEAP at the chance. You would be a fool not to. This opportunity doesn't come around every day and to think that it will be here in the following years is foolish. With the way the industry is going, you had better capitalize on the opportunity today before it's gone tomorrow.

Controlling your destiny is not an opportunity that comes by every day. In this instance you not only have the choice of how much you produce, you also have the choice of how much you work. How fucking great is that? It all comes down to how ambitious you are feeling.

Let this be a positive word of warning. If you decide to put it into overdrive and go for three harvests you need to understand this from the get go: you are going to work. This ain't no "hit it and quit it" or "set it and forget it" endeavor. You will have to work. Not only work, but work on a schedule. Your time will be regulated for approximately 8 months. You will have to set a daily routine and stick to it. The good news is the payoff is huge, you will be working for yourself, and all that sweat and effort you expend will be rewarded.

When the time comes and you start covering, you will want to cover at the same time every day. And when you uncover you will have to uncover at the same time every day. Same with watering, you want to water at the same time of day every time you water.

The more you schedule and set to a routine the easier things will become because repetition will make you memorize what you should and need to be doing. So you will be faster and more efficient without quality suffering. The time you free up by becoming efficient will probably be spent looking around and making sure that everything is just so. Looking for problem spots or potential problems. By spotting potential problems and fixing them you end up saving yourself tons of time and save yourself a potential loss in the garden.

Choosing to do light deprivation means you get to choose your seasons. You are no longer bound to the whims of nature and her seasons. Spring doesn't have to be just spring anymore, it could be your summer. And summer? Why summer could be your fall. The choices are many and you get to choose what season your plants experience when you want them too. Meaning no disrespect to Mother Nature, we the planet need all of her seasons. But you as a grower do not. You only need summer and fall. So you have the benefit of choosing when those two seasons are going to occur.

By harvesting in June/July you get to avoid all sorts of potential problems. Namely the law and rip-offs. Those pesky problems usually arrive way later in the season. However, if for some reason Johnny Law comes a calling early in the season and pulls your plants the game is not over. There is usually enough time to start over. You will probably be able to replant. The government pretty much has a budget for one visit per year. They have other fish to fry on their grand tour and can't circle back again and again. They don't have the budget to do more than that.

More than likely they will come later in the season when your plants are bigger. They like the bigger plants because they look more impressive when they make their reports to the local news agencies. The two things the law likes during a bust are huge plants or a lot of plants because when they make their report to higher-ups they can say: "See how many there were?" or "Look how big they are? We are being effective- give us more money please!" Fortunately for you, you will already have pulled a harvest and have some money in the ground. This will help with your whole outlook on life, let me tell you.

Rip-offs on the other hand never come sniffing around in July, unless they already know where you live and your schedule. Which is a scary thought but a necessary precaution. Make sure you trust the people you share your information with. Other than that, you are pretty safe from rip-offs in July. Those good for nothings are at home watching their TVs waiting for October to come around so they can mount up and plan a raid. Believe it or not, this really does happen so be prudent and put the proper safe guards in place. This is another great reason to do light dep! Plan your harvests correctly and you have a real chance of avoiding the whole scene. Having the peace of mind this gives you is worth all the extra planning and work. Especially when you are sitting on the beach with a drink in your hand in the middle of October!

Failure sucks but there is a difference between failure and COMPLETE FAILURE. There are an unlimited amount of reasons for failure. 99.9% of them can be avoided if you have the right plan. Avoiding complete failure is fairly easy to do even when you only have a mediocre plan. Believe it or not, the difference between failure and success is not much. You put in about the same amount of work. Only the end result is different. That is why we want to harvest two or three times a year. It helps to avoid failure and speeds us to success.

So let's focus on succeeding! The only way to get ahead in this business is to hustle and have multiple harvests in a calendar year. You can't afford to put all your eggs in one basket. Too much depends on you succeeding. You need to be able to put food on the table, keep a roof over your head and pay the bills. Learning how to light dep is like getting the Keys to the Kingdom. You will be able to overcome any temporary failures with the successes that quickly follow.

Reusing the grow space you have will make you so much money- and save you money at the same time! The great part is you only have to set the space up once. Once all the work of setting it up is done, and I admit it is quite a bit of work, that's it. You don't have to go through setting up something else. Hauling in all that soil, running water line, filling pots.... Now you get the benefit of all that hard work by reusing that spot over and over again in one year. You, my friend, are going green by using the three R's: Reduce, Reuse, and Recycle. You can become very successful following this routine!

Maybe you only have a small area to work with. If you only have a small area then you are almost obligated to do light dep. There is only so much yield an area can give. No matter how many tricks and techniques you use there is only so much a space can give. The only way to get more out of your space is to do multiple harvests. It doesn't hurt that you make more money doing it and get to actually save money by not having to set up something from scratch. It almost seems unfair.

Even if you have a large space that is already set up and relatively flat you should seriously consider doing light dep because the hardest part (the setup) is already done.

The overall workload for three harvests is fairly big. The great news is the work is staggered over time. You won't be facing a giant mountain of work at any one point, unless you are starting from scratch. Setting everything up the first time is a lot of work, no doubt. If you are already set up the biggest workdays will be harvesting and replanting. Good news there, since you are working with smaller plants it still won't be that hard, but you will have to put in some hours.

Light dep is a great way to make the most of your growing space. You are able run many cycles in the same place and reuse your soil over and over again. With the proper knowledge you will be able to maximize your growing space without having to break the bank by expanding. And expanding again.

That is the temptation in this business: to keep expanding. The thinking goes "Oh I produced this much this year, next year I can produce this much if I expand over there. That cycle of that thinking never stops. If you are prone to that thinking, it will keep nagging at you no matter what you do.

Well, instead of expanding to make more you could just use the light dep technique to produce more, without increasing your footprint. The more you expand the bigger the fish you become. The bigger the fish you become the tastier you look when the law decides to make visits. So instead of expanding your garden size maybe you are better off doing some light dep and staying a small fish. Well, actually you will only LOOK like a small fish when in actuality you are a biggish fish. Hope that helps those of you out there that want to be the big fish.

Weather in the summer is wonderful. Warm and sunny skies, these are the things that all gardeners dream of. Did you know that the summer weather brings more benefits than just warm weather and sunny skies? The summer weather is less humid and the sun has a higher intensity. What does this mean for the light dep gardener? It means more money and less potential problems.

Because the summer weather is drier than in the winter months (well at least in California) there are less mold spores in the air. Less mold spores in the air mean a smaller chance of getting mold in your plants. When doing light dep, potential mold problems are one of the major battles that must be contended with. So harvesting in the summer is great because your plants finish faster and have less of a chance of becoming infected by mold.

In the summer the sun is closer to the surface of the Earth because of the tilt of the Earth's axis. What does this mean to you? It means the sunlight is more intense. This increased intensity means the plants grow faster, bigger and produce more THC. By harvesting in summer you end up with a bigger, better yield that is far superior to the fall crop!

Cycling your harvests through the year allows you to spread the workload out over time. A normal long season workload looks like this: In spring you have a lot of work to get started. You have to plant your plants, make sure they are warm and you need to test everything to make sure it is working (that's really just the tip of the iceberg). In summer you have a very light workload. You just have routine maintenance to do. In the fall you have a massive amount of work to do. You have to prepare your dry room, harvest everything in waves, and make sure that everything is running smoothly.

Now if you do light dep your workload is spread out over six to seven months. You never get that down time in summer because you are harvesting and preparing your next run. But you are never stuck under a mountain of work either. Yes, you will be harvesting the same amount, if not more per run, but you get to harvest the whole thing at once. This allows you to become very efficient because all you have to do is cut down the plant. You don't have to look it over and wonder if this part of the plant is ready for harvest like you do with big plants.

Make no mistake the turnover rate of harvests will mean you have less work per run, simply because of the shortened season. The shortened season increases turnover and reduces maintenance.

This means you won't be wasting your time growing stems. Growing stems what happens when you grow big plants. Your plant is growing up and out to reach more light. The plant is trying to cover as much area as possible in the limited time it is given. By using light dep techniques you are growing significantly smaller plants that will yield just as much as the big plant in a fraction of the time. If you have dreams of growing giant plants light dep is not for you. The whole point is to increase turnover and the only way to do that is with smaller plants.

Another factor to consider is maintenance. Maintaining a small plant is a whole hell of a lot easier than trying to maintain a big plant. With a small plant you are able to reach everywhere you need by hand. You don't need any ladders, step stools, or special gear to reach the plants. Yeah- it sounds cool and looks cool when you see a giant plant. But let me tell you maintaining a big plant is a giant pain in the ass. If you only have one or two no problem, but what do you do if you have 60 or 70? You are now spending 4 to 5 hours a day making sure they are okay. And the closer you get to harvest the more time you spend with them.

When you are dealing with big plants these are the things that you need to do to maintain them: You need to stake them up. Put a cage around each one. As they get bigger you will need to support the branches because they will get so heavy that they break. Now you've got to clean the inside of the plant out. This means you need to go into the interior of the plant and cut out all the branches and leaves that are not getting direct sunlight. If you don't, those branches will just sap the energy away from the branches and buds that do get light. Okay you cleaned out the interior now what? In about three weeks you will have to go through and do it again. Really? Yes, really! These plants, when given ideal conditions, grow at a phenomenal rate. And you of course are going to give them ideal conditions, right? Now you have to go through again and tie up some more branches because they are now too heavy.

Whew- now it's harvest time! So you pull out your ladder and harvest the outside of the plant and let the interior finish up. It will be ready in a week or two! By growing big plants you have effectively tripled or quadrupled your work load per harvest! That's crazy as there is no reason for it unless your plants are on some steep terrain. All that time wasted on maintenance. That is time you could be doing something else and earning more.

Finding help in the off season is a lot easier than trying to find help in October. In October there are so many people harvesting, drying and trimming that it is hard to find help. Everyone is already busy helping someone else. If you plan ahead you will be able to find willing help in a snap.

When you harvest in the summer it is fairly easy to find some quick help to do the harvesting, replanting and trimming. There are always a few people that you know that need to earn a quick buck. And since it is summer they aren't doing anything else so you can snatch them up! They are doing you a favor and you are doing them a favor. Just make sure to line up two or three people because sometimes your number one option falls through.

And if you are really on your game (and after reading this book you should be) you will be able to schedule an early fall harvest. If you harvest in mid September you will still have beat the market and be able to find help. It's just like driving in the big city. There are times that are easy to drive through the city and times when the traffic is gridlocked. So plan ahead!

Planning ahead is the only way to pull off a triple harvest in one year. This doesn't happen by accident. You need to have a clear plan that is detailed down to the T. Next up is the execution of that plan. A plan is meaningless without the gumption to execute it. How many people do you know who talk a good game only to fail when it comes to getting off their ass to do something about it? I know more than a 100 of those people and so do you! Don't fall prey to that voice in your head that tells you that you have plenty of time, you can get started later. Guess what? It's later than you think and you better get to hustling if you want to achieve your goals. Success requires a clear plan and some serious execution.

Developing your plan is a process that needs to be taken seriously. Even if you got this book in the middle of the season you should still develop a plan. The developing of your plan will help you establish goals and help you to communicate more effectively with yourself and others. It will help you to stop deluding yourself and telling yourself that you have all the time in the world. I'm here to tell you that you don't. Before you know it a year will have gone by. If you are on your game in that year you will have accomplished a lot!

Take the time out of your busy schedule to plan your season because, honestly, you are planning more than just your season of work. You are planning for your future success and the lifestyle you want to lead. The time you take to make your plan WILL be the difference between being successful and achieving your dreams or failing. The plan you are about to write will not only lay out your schedule but should seriously motivate you to achieve those goals! Just think of all those milestones that you will hit and all the rewards that go with it. Shit, I'm excited for you just thinking about it!

So get on your ass (yes, I said 'ON' your ass- sit down), do some serious research (like reading this book) and put pen to paper. Establish your goals and calculate how to achieve them. This book will lead you most of the way there. But ultimately *you* need to plan the race and run it. I can't do it for you and I wouldn't want to (I've got my own races to run).

In summary:

Light dep is for everyone. It is for the absolute beginner AND the experienced grower. Light dep is not rocket science- even though it has a lot of science backing it up. In fact, I would say light dep is pretty easy to do when you have the right information backing you up. The people who will benefit the most from it are the savvy ones who understand what light dep is offering you. This is more than just a technique that I am teaching you. This is a chance to take control of your life and change your life for good. This is a chance to make your life go from okay to great. To grasp the reigns and turn your life in the direction you want to go.

Uninformed people think that doing light dep is not for them. They probably think it is harder than it is and takes an extraordinary amount of work to get it done. You and I both know that is not the case. Light dep does take a little more work than long season, but you end up with double to triple the yield. So the extra work is worth it.

Most people who know about light dep but still refuse to do it tend to be in two categories: people who are stuck and people who are afraid.

People who are stuck are the kind of people who say things like "This is the way I've always done and I ain't changing for you or no one." I know a few of those people and I'm sure you do too. Another version is "light dep can't be that good because I'm not doing it." They may be stuck on not having enough information, lacking a guide on how to do it, or any number of things. Don't fall into this trap. You can do this and we both know it ain't that hard.

People who are afraid are a different breed altogether. They may be afraid for any number of reasons. Such as "what if I fail" or "I'm not good at trying new things" or "that sounds complicated/ too much work"…. The list goes on and on.

Frankly, we don't have the time to go over all the reasons why these people won't do light dep. And really it's not our business. We are in the business of succeeding and getting shit done. I assume that is why you are reading this book.

In no particular order let's go over the reasons why you should do light dep:

-You get to choose how much you will work, when you will work and work for yourself
-You get to maximize the space you have already created.
-You can harvest early and have an early year.
-You get to command the seasons!
-Last, but certainly not least, you get to decide how much you will produce.

2 WHAT IS LIGHT DEP?

Light deprivation, or light dep for short, means artificially simulating some of the fall conditions. How do you artificially simulate fall conditions? This is easily done by restricting your plant's access to sunlight. You do this by covering the plant with a piece of material that is lightproof over a rigid frame. So in essence you are shortening the "days" and lengthening the "nights". Why would you want to do this? You do this to force your plants to start flowering earlier in the season. By starting the flowering process earlier in the year it allows you to pull off one or more runs per season while the weather is great.

The idea is to cover the plant so it is exposed to 12 or more hours of uninterrupted dark. The uninterrupted dark is what triggers the plant into flowering. Flowering is the plant's way of reproducing and securing the next generation of the species. With the shortening of the days the plant understands that winter is coming and must rapidly produce as many flowers as possible in order to produce seed before the winter sets in. The flower is the promise of the next generation. Unfortunately for the plant, but fortunately for you, there will be no seed. The female flowers will not be pollinated. Instead you will just have beautiful, sticky, stinky bud. As the saying goes: "the stickiest of the sticky and the ickiest of the icky!"

Old technology commandeered by a renegade industry is exactly what light dep is. The flower industry has been using the light deprivation technique for decades. How do you think you get all those wonderful flowers in the middle of summer? You know, the ones that only naturally flower in fall? Unless you are in the flower industry you probably have never even given it a second thought. You probably figured the plants were just naturally flowering somewhere in the world and were shipped to your local flower shop. While that might be true for some varieties it's not true for all varieties of flowers. Those beautiful fall flowers that you saw in the stores or at your local florist last summer were brought to you by none other than light deprivation techniques that were invented by the flower industry to make a buck. And not just a little buck. We are talking millions annually. Here is your opportunity to use their scientifically proven techniques to help you get ahead.

Don't be mistaken. This is not some new fly by night technique that is unproven. This has scientific backing by a multi-million dollar a year industry. Those fat cats don't play when it comes to their money. So if they are using this proven technology you should too. They know something that you may not. Harvesting multiple times a year makes you better-off. The best part about this opportunity is that they put in all that money to do the research and you get use that million dollar research for the cost of this book!

Scheduling when to cover and when to uncover is the very basis of light dep. Cover too long and you don't get the yield you should have (not to mention the risk of getting diseases). Cover for too short of a period and you end up with giant plants and no flowers. Both of those techniques are a massive waste of time and resources. You need to cover your plants for a certain amount of uninterrupted hours of darkness or everything you have done is for not.

While there is an exact amount time you should be covering the plants that exact amount is a range. The range of time the plants should be exposed to uninterrupted darkness is 12 to 14 hours of darkness. This is very important. If you are only exposing your plants to 11 hours of darkness they will probably flower (depending on the variety you choose to use) but they will take forever to finish. Heck, they might not even finish at all. You could have harvested your plants in 8 to 10 weeks using the 12 hours of darkness technique (depending on the variety) and instead it took you 10 to 12 weeks because you only gave your plants 11 hours of darkness. Yes, you may end up with more weight but the quality of bud would be diminished. Instead of tight nice nuggets you will have stretched out squaffy buds. Not at all what you want! Not even remotely close.

By adhering to the fairly flexible time range for covering your plants you will be rewarded with a beautiful crop that finishes in a timely manner. Namely 8 to 10 weeks depending on the variety.

Not all light dep techniques are the same even though to the uninitiated the may seem the same. Depping (slang for light dep) inside a greenhouse is known as black box. This is not the same as a regular light dep. The results are pretty much the same but the technique is different.

Most people don't know the difference between the two and use the terms light dep and black box interchangeably. There are subtle differences and some not so subtle differences. I can positively guarantee you that they are NOT the same and if you used light dep techniques and only light dep techniques on a black box situation you would be very disappointed in the results. And vice versa is true too.

Regular light dep is done outside with a frame. The plants are exposed to the elements. This comes with a whole host of benefits and drawbacks that we will cover later in this book.

Black box is doing light dep inside a greenhouse. The plants are protected from the elements by the greenhouse. This also comes with a host of benefits and drawbacks as well. Again, this will be covered in more detail in a later chapter.

Now you know the essential difference between the two techniques. If someone tells you that they are the same, you can say that in fact they are not the same. If you want, you could actually explain the differences and wow your audience into silence! Probably not, but you never know.

If you are a beginner your learning curve will be steep, but not because of using the light dep technique. Your curve will be steep because of all the growing techniques and plant knowledge you are going to learn & implement in a short period of time.

One thing to keep in mind as a beginner is this: if you learn a great technique, that technique may not be able to scale up. Huh? This means that if a particular technique will work on a small scale, it may not work on a large scale. There are a number of reasons techniques won't scale up to larger scales. They usually fall in these categories: too expensive, too much work, wasteful, or impossible to implement on a large scale. For our purposes, I have found that the number one reason is it would be too much work to implement. Now, I'm not afraid of some hard work, but your plate is already loaded. You don't need to go finding extra work. Trust me you already have enough!

As an experienced grower these techniques will be a cinch for you to implement. You already have the plant knowledge which is the hardest to attain. You have already made the mistakes and learned the hard way. All you need now is the light dep knowledge and techniques that are covered in this book.

Now all you have to do is start. Starting is how you decide when to finish. Your start date is whenever you choose it to be, according to the yearly goals that you set. You get to chose when you work and how much you work. You get to decide your workload! I put an exclamation point there because that is some exciting shit! There did I it again.

Just stop and think about it for a serious minute. You get to choose how many runs you do. You get to decide your workload. If you wanted to you could decide that you want to only do one run and call it good. Can you imagine getting started in April and finishing in July? Seriously think of the advantages! You get your starts. Then you grow them to the right size. Next you pull tarp for 2 months and voila you're done. You harvest, hang it and dry it. Then you get it trimmed and that's it. All done. Now you have 8 more months to play until you have to start working again. In the meantime go to the beach and have a drink. Think about that. That is a game changer if I have ever heard of one- and it's yours to choose.

And if you are more motivated? You plan for that.

So you decided that one harvest isn't going to quite do it for you? Well what about two? No? Then how about three? Surely three will be enough! You've bitten off a big piece but it is completely manageable with planning.

With three harvests you will be working for 8 months straight. That doesn't mean you won't get breaks. Of course you will. You will still get weekends off in the beginning. You can even get weekends off in the middle if you plan accordingly.

Since you are going to be working for 8 months you can decide when you want to finish. Do you want to finish in October or do you want to finish in November? If you decide to finish in October you should start in February. If you chose to finish in November then you should start in March. The truth is, if you are on top of your game you could start in March and finish in October. Only if you are on the top of your game should you attempt this. Otherwise take a little more time and make sure to get it right.

You not only get to choose when those two seasons occur you get to choose where they are going to occur. They could be in your back yard any day this year or next. The choice is up to you. Don't let the choices you get to make stop there. You also get to choose whether you will produce a little or if you will produce a lot, whether you get to live a comfy life or a life of luxury. So many choices you get to make and choosing when summer and fall occur is one of them.

3 CHOOSING A LOCATION FOR YOUR STRUCTURE

When you decide to build your light dep structure there are several things to consider. The most important thing to consider that covers the broadest range of parameters is this: where should you locate your light dep structure for success? Let's define success as pulling off a good harvest with the least amount of effort necessary. With that in mind the three main things you need to consider when deciding on a location: is it accessible? does it have enough privacy? is it getting enough sun?

When you are building your structure you want ease of access. You will have to build it yourself and hauling load after load by hand gets tiring. If you get tired and decide that "fuck it this is too much work" then you have located your structure in a shitty spot. End of story. Find a spot you can drive up to real close.

You will definitely want to consider the path of the sun when you build your structure. If the location you choose is shady you will want to cut in some light. I recommend topping your trees not removing them. Or move your structure to a sunnier spot. The goal is to give your plants 12 hours of great sun so keep that in mind when you choose your location.

The last consideration is privacy. You will want you structure to be private. This means people can't see it off the road as they drive by. If you can achieve that, great! If not you will have to either block it from view or step up security to prevent rip-offs.

The ground on which you choose to build should be somewhat level. It is okay if it is gently sloped. The structure should be oriented with the length running in the direction of the slope. If that is confusing what I am trying to say is the longer length of the structure should run in the direction of the slope.

This is important because you will be pulling plastic up and over your frames. By having the long side of the structure running parallel to the direction of the slope you won't have a "high" side and a "low" side when pulling the plastic over the frame. This will make it easier to actually pull the plastic over your frames.

Now, it is okay if you can't build the structure in that direction because the hillside is too steep. It will still work. You will just have a harder time covering and uncovering. Don't let that worry you too much. Don't let that deter you. You will still be able to get the job done, so carry on.

If for some reason you don't have any relatively flat land you may need to have some tractor work done. If you are going to get tractor work done, make sure to check your local laws on grading. It is best to get tractor work done in the winter so you can spread grass seed down. The winter rains will sprout the seed and cover up any tractor work as well as stabilize the hillside. If you have to do the tractor work in the spring or summer make sure to put down hay to protect the hillside.

When you are setting up your structure or when you are doing any major project you must think of your future self. Think of how much work you are giving your future self. When you think of it in that way it makes setting stuff up easier. If you don't know what I mean, all you need to do is ask yourself, "What would my future self want? Is my future self going to hate me because I set it up this way?" If the answer is yes, or maybe, then you will want to reconsider your current plans and create plans with your future self in mind.

For example, "Is there water access where you are setting up the structure?" If the only water access is to haul in water by hand you should seriously reconsider your garden location. If you can't relocate the garden, then you are going to need to build a system to get water to your garden. Because hauling water is not an option if you are going big.

Maybe you will have to place a water tank at a higher elevation than the garden and run water line to the garden. If that is what you need to do then do it. You don't want to add to your workload if at all possible, because you will have plenty already. And if for some reason your future self gets lazy and doesn't to water because he doesn't want to haul water by hand you could be in some serious trouble. Plan ahead.

Ease of use will guarantee your success. You will be able to set a routine that will allow you to get the job done faster. The faster you get the job done in a quality fashion the more you can relax and pay attention to the things that really matter. Like the health and well being of your plants.

All of these benefits come from considering where you are going to place your structure. The only cost is the time spent thinking. Of course you won't be able to anticipate every problem that springs up with your location. Fixing the problem should always be considered in the same way as locating your structure. This time though you should ask yourself: "Is this going to cause more work for my future self or is this going fix it permanently?"

You should always try to find a permanent solution if possible. I understand that it is not always possible. Sometimes the solution is too expensive or the materials aren't available. If you are really lucky the problem will occur near the end of your run and hopefully it won't really matter. I know because it has happened to friends many, many times. In those cases you just do what you can and hope for the best.

Preplanning your structure and working on your layout will speed up the construction process. Spend the time thinking and planning the location of the structure and how you are going to build it. You will run into snags when building your structure no matter how much you plan ahead. Do you want to spend your time out in the field trying to figure out those snags? Or do you want to sit at home and plan ahead to avoid those snags?

Personally, I prefer the planning ahead option. You waste less time out in the field when you grab a piece of paper and a pencil and PLAN. The planning of your structure should cover just about every aspect of the process. This isn't rocket science, but a plan will save you hours and hours of wasted time. If you don't know how to develop a plan to build something and avoid snags that's okay. You are about to learn.

Choosing the area of your structure is a very important process that has some constraints that need to be considered. Namely the area/size, practicality and availability of materials.

The area constraint is always bound on the bigger size, not the smaller. When you build a small structure you have all the materials available to you with no problems. However, if you decide to build a big structure you will run into some problems. You will probably have to custom order parts or buy standard sizes that are way too big. Custom ordering is always more expensive than standard sizes because the manufacturer has to change the settings on the machines. If you don't custom order you end up getting the standard size and then you will have to cut your materials to the size you need which leads to a lot of waste. Not to mention all the time spent custom fitting the material to the size of your structure. This whole industry is filled with scenarios just like this.

Just because you have a huge area that you can work with doesn't mean that you can or should build a structure to cover the whole area. Instead you may want to build two structures. Sometimes building two structures is just easier and faster. While building two structures may be (but not necessarily) more expensive than building one, it is far more practical and user friendly. Not to mention you will be able to purchase your materials with ease.

Now, I have built bigger structures and used them as light deps. I ran into several problems that I did not anticipate. These are the problems I ran into: Covering the structure was a bitch because it was so tall. It took at least 20 minutes to cover the damn thing while yanking as hard as I could. I also had to pay extra for the dep tarp because it was a custom size. I had to add extra support to the frames because of the load I was putting on them. I spent hours repairing the plastic and frames. Hours and hours of wasted time that would have been better spent building two structures.

Trust me, make a smaller structure that is standard size so you can manage it by yourself.

The height of the structure will determine how tall you can grow your plants. You don't want your plants to grow too tall because they can be damaged by the plastic as it is pulled over the frame. Another consideration is the taller your plants are the more heat they will experience. This is because heat rises and when trapped in a "room" it goes to the top first and then slowly fills the room from the top down. Think of it like a sealed room that is being filled by water. You know how it fills from the bottom up? Well heat does the same thing, except opposite. Heat fills from the top down. So the taller your plants are the sooner they will experience the heat when covered.

Now heat is a good thing when it is in a certain range. Outside of that range it can have catastrophic effects on your plants. So try to keep your plants fairly short.

There are several ways to keep you plants short. You can tie them down to keep them low. You can pinch them to encourage lateral growth. You can even top them if they get too tall (NOT DURING FLOWER!). By keeping your plants short you are avoiding future problems that will occur.

4 BUILDING YOUR OWN LIGHT DEP GREENHOUSE

Kit structures have many advantages over the Do It Yourself method. The kit is usually an all inclusive package with instructions. So it should be easy to set up. What's nice about kits is you pay for it and your shopping is essentially done. You don't have to make a list, check it twice and then run around and buy all the materials. Of course kits tend to be more expensive than a DIY, but you do save time which is important.

Usually the design of a kit is all inclusive and they tell you what is not included so you can easily go to the store to pick up what is missing. The importance of this can't be overstated. You get to avoid so many hassles by using a kit. The drawback of course is the price. Now sometimes, but not often, you run into a kit that was poorly designed. Someone just slapped some stuff together, called it a kit and put it up for sale. YOU need to do your research if you are going to buy a kit. So do it- and the end result will have been worth the effort of sitting on your computer and making a few calls!

If you don't have the money for a fancy kit, never fear you can create an excellent light dep structure on your own. The DIY/budget method is how light dep was invented! People didn't go out and buy light dep kits. Back in the day they made them from scratch by themselves. What worked back then still works today. Lucky you.

Because you are making the structure yourself out of materials from the store, the structure tends to be a little weaker than a fancy kit. This is not an issue. All we need is a frame that will hold the plastic up and off of the plants. We are talking about a plastic sheet. Not very heavy unless you try to lift it up all at once all by yourself. Since we aren't, the weight load is an almost nonissue. Your frame ribs only have to hold up less than 10 pounds each. The frame will experience far more load from you pulling the plastic over them than they will from the weight of the plastic itself.

You will never guess what the growers of old, and even today, use as their frame structure. They use one inch PVC pipes that are 20 feet long. This length of pipe will make a hoop or rib anywhere from 8 to 12 feet wide depending on how you lay it out. And to anchor it? Why 3 foot sections of 5/8 inch rebar. You hammer in the rebar halfway (18 inches) down into the ground and do another one 8 to 12 feet away. Then you place the PVC over the rebar stakes that are sticking up and you now have a rib. Easy day.

Supporting the plastic is the purpose of the ribs. They need to be laid out in such a way as to achieve this goal. You need to do an initial layout so that the ribs will be laid out in a straight line. The straighter the line the stronger the ribs will be. This will make sure that the plants are properly protected from the dep tarp. You will also have to not only consider how wide you want your ribs but how far apart the ribs are from each other.

The standard spacing for ribs is 4 to 6 feet apart. I recommend using the 4 feet method if you're outside and the 6 feet method if you're in a greenhouse. Now all you have to do is choose which distance to use and set your budget.

Here are some great benefits of using PVC: It is inexpensive, easy to work with, 20 foot lengths have a "bell" on them so you can easily extend the length if you want. If you use 20 foot lengths as your rib you know the distance over your greenhouse is 20 feet! I personally recommend using PVC for the beginner because it is so easy to work with and very forgiving.

Now that you have decided to put your ribs up you need to stabilize them. To stabilize the ribs you need to connect them all to each other. The way to do this is using a purlin. A purlin is a straight pole that is continuous and the length of the ribs. The purlin is attached to each rib. For light dep you want to make sure that the purlin is located on the inside of the ribs. This way when the plastic is pulled over the ribs it does not catch on the purlin. The best location for a purlin on a small hoop house is located at the peak of the rib. Again the purlin should be on the inside of the ribs NOT the outside.

Purlins are very effective at their jobs. When you use a PVC rib it is very flimsy and sways side to side with little effort even though it is attached to the ground at two points. Once the purlin is attached to each rib the whole structure becomes pretty rigid. I recommend using the same size PVC you used to make the ribs as the material you use to make the purlin.

The easiest way to attach the purlin to the ribs is duct tape- really! Duct tape is cheap and easy to use. Small rope or zip ties are okay as well, so long as the knots are on the inside of the rib so as not to rip the plastic as it is pulled over the frame. I do not recommend using wire because it has a tendency to catch and rip the plastic over time.

The great thing about using this method is you can get these materials from most any hardware store, lumber yard, or plumbing supply. They will usually have everything you need in stock. So you don't have to make any special orders or make extra trips to the store.

Before you go to the store make sure you take the time to make a list of all the things you need. That way you can get everything at once and save yourself the headaches and hassles of running around.

To create a materials list figure out how long you want your structure to be. Then you figure you are going to place ribs every 4 feet. So for every rib you need 2 pieces of rebar. Then you also want to figure out how much PVC you need for the purlin.

Here is a quick example illustrating how to create a materials list:

Suppose we are building a 40 foot by 10 foot hoop house. We are going to use 20 foot lengths of 1 inch Schedule 40 (that is a measurement of the pipe wall thickness) PVC spaced at 4 foot intervals. So we divide 40 feet by 4 feet and we get 10. So that means we need 10 ribs, right? Wrong. We need 11 ribs because you need an extra one for the starting location. So we need 11 pieces of PVC for the ribs and 22 pieces of rebar for the anchors for the ribs. For the purlins we divide 40 feet by 20 feet, which gives us 2. So we need 2 pieces of PVC for the purlins. That's a total of 13 pieces of PVC.

Quick recap: figure out the length of your structure and divide that number by 4 and add 1 to the total. This is the number of ribs you need. To figure out how many anchors you need multiply the number of ribs by 2. For the length of the purlins divide the length of the structure by 20. If you get a decimal when calculating for the purlin round up, no matter how small the decimal is.

And if you're a math nerd like me here are quick calculations for the quantity of materials:

$A = (X/4) + 1$ where:
$B = A(2)$ A = # of ribs you need C = length of purlins
$C = X/20$ B = # of rebar anchors you need X = desired length of structure (ft)

5 CHOOSING THE RIGHT LIGHT DEP TARP

Light proof is the basic requirement for the plastic that is used to cover your light dep. There are many properties that should be considered when you decide to purchase your plastic. But the one that needs to be considered first and foremost is: is it light proof? The second most important one is: will it cover the frame completely with about two feet of excess on all the sides? You think I'm joking but I, and many others, have fallen prey to these common problems. So make sure you check first. This will save you time and money, guaranteed.

You need to make sure when purchasing plastic that you ask someone if this plastic is indeed light proof. Better yet bring a powerful flashlight and try to shine the light through. If the light doesn't shine through you are probably going to be okay. Make sure it isn't some crappy light that barely puts out any light! Your whole dep future is counting on your plastic being light proof. I remember one time I had purchased a big ass dep tarp and to make sure it was light proof I crawled into it when it was midday and I had my friend seal it up around my legs. Guess what? I couldn't see one iota of light and that was how I knew it was light proof.

When purchasing light dep plastic 5.5 mil is the minimum thickness that you want to use for light dep plastic. I mean the minimum! Any thinner than that and you are seriously risking light leaks. Now you may be wondering what a mil is. A mil is one thousandth of an inch. In decimals that is 0.001 inches thick. As you can see it is very thin and 5.5mil is not very thick at all. Now the maximum thickness you want is 12mil. That is a fairly thick piece of plastic that has a lot of weight to it.

The thicker your plastic gets the harder it is to pull because the plastic increases in weight as the thickness increases. Thicker plastic also costs more because you are getting more material. Now I don't want to deter you from getting thicker plastic because thicker plastic definitely has benefits. Such as (but not limited to): better light proofing, durability and less susceptible to being blown about.

The thinner your plastic is the less durable it is and it is more likely to rip when being pulled over the frame. Thinner plastic also has its own set of benefits such as (but not limited to): easier to pull, costs less and easier to handle because of its pliable nature.

Thickness is the dependent variable in how much your plastic is going to weigh. The size, of course, also plays a key role in how much your light dep tarp is going to weigh. When using plastic in the 6mil to 12mil range the weight will be in the range of 4oz/sy to 8.5oz/sy respectively. If you are wondering what an oz/sy is let me break it down for you. The oz part is short for ounces (weight) and the sy is short for square yard (area).

Now the way that you use this information is simple. For my fellow math nerds out there let's start with an equation:

$$W=A(P)$$

where:
W= weight of the tarp (oz)
A = area of the tarp is square yards (sy)
P = average weight if the tarp in ounces per square yard (oz/sy)

Here is a quick example. Let's say you have a light dep tarp that is 6 mil thick and is 18 feet by 42 feet. First you convert the feet into yards (3 feet per yard). This yields an area of 6 yards by 14 yards. Now you multiply 6 yards by 14 yards which equals 84 square yards or 84sy. Now we take that 84sy and multiply that by 4 oz/yd. This equals 336 ounces which we convert to pounds by dividing it by 16 ounces. The 18 feet by 42 feet tarp will weigh a total of 21 pounds!

This is important to know because if you do a manual dep YOU are going to be maneuvering this giant sheet of plastic around by yourself. So you are going to want to know beforehand if it weighs too much before purchasing it.

Durability of your light dep plastic is a serious consideration. Not only for the job at hand but for your pocketbook. Durability of the plastic is dependent on a lot of factors. The major ones that concern us are the thickness, handling technique, frames and UV protection.

Now we have already gone over the thickness aspect of the plastic. Long and short of it is, the thicker the plastic is the more durable it will be and the thinner the plastic is the less durable it will be.

Next up are the handling technique that you use to pull the plastic over your frames. It is always wise to develop a covering/uncovering technique that requires the minimum amount of force possible. That being said, sometimes you'll have to yank the dickens out of the plastic to get it to go over the frames. This is especially true if your frames are taller than your reach! So if that is the case you had best develop a strategy that will insure the longevity of your tarp. These may include a: a step stool, rope, someone tall, a pole attached to the plastic, pulleys... The list could go on and on. It is only limited by your imagination.

Lastly, we come we come to UV protection.

UV treated light dep tarp is one of the major key components to the longevity of your tarp. If the plastic is indeed treated it will definitely make your plastic last longer. The sun is a harsh mistress and will destroy plastic in nothing flat. I know it doesn't seem like that is the case but if your plastic is not treated it will turn brittle and fall apart in a year or so. I personally have experienced this and it sucked. Not only did it cut short the lifespan of my plastic that I paid my hard earned money for, it left a nasty mess that I had to clean up! Can you imagine picking up a tarp that literally falls to pieces? You don't want to deal with that.

The good news is most plastic is treated with some sort of UV protection. This will get you anywhere from 2 to 4 years of use. The even better news is that rating is for plastic that is left in the sun 24 hours a day, 7 days a week. You know for 2 to 4 years straight. If you are doing your part you are only using your plastic maybe 6 months out of the year. So this means your plastic should last anywhere from 4 to 8 years. That is of course based on the wild speculation that you are taking care of it.

So if your plastic is 6 mil and UV treated and you use it 6 months out of the year it could last for 4 years. I say *could* because the reality definitely falls somewhat short of that timeframe. The thing that needs to be considered is that nature of pulling the tarp over a frame twice a day for essentially 120 days a year is inherently destructive. The truth is the plastic was not designed to do that. It was designed to be tossed over something, like hay or silage, in the middle of a field somewhere with the ends tucked in so as not to blow around and left alone for an extended period of time. That's why it is 6 mils thick! It's meant to be used to cover something and be left alone.

Now if you have a dep tarp that is 12 mil and UV treated and is used 6 months out of the year it could definitely last anywhere from 4 to 6 years with the proper care. Of course 12 mil is some heavy duty plastic and a bit of a pain in the ass to use by hand, but you can count on it to be there for you that's for sure!

There are basically two different types of plastic that are used for light dep tarps. They are plastic film and polywoven plastic.

The plastic film is also known as sheeting, or blow molded plastic. Basically this plastic is one continuous piece of plastic. It is similar to saran wrap. You notice how on saran wrap there are no splices? It's just one long piece of plastic that just starts at the beginning and ends at the end. The same is true for plastic film. They use a machine that heats plastic up and uses forced air to produce the plastic into one continuous sheet. No joins or anything.

Another thing about plastic film is it tends to be in the range of 4 mils to 8 mils thick. While plastic film can be thicker, it is less common than the thinner varieties. You will sometimes see 10 mil plastic and almost never 12 mil plastic (at least for dep tarps). The most commonly used film in the industry is the thinner variety in the range of 6 mil to 8 mil which is a lot easier to use due to its lighter weight.

Now the polywoven plastic is a bird of a different feather. Poly is short for polyethylene (which is very common type of plastic). The woven part is because it is actually woven. Have you ever looked up close at one of those blue tarps? You ever notice that it is woven with tiny fibers. Well that is an example of polywoven plastic. The benefit of using polywoven tarps is durability. If somehow you get a rip in your tarp (which you let me tell you, you will!) the hole it creates won't run. The hole will stop from running like a nylon stocking because the unripped fibers at edge will maintain their integrity. This will save you a lot of work in the long run.

Reinforced plastic is another version of plastic film. The tarp is made in layers. The layers are as follows: the outer layer, the reinforcement layer, and the inner layer.

The outer layer is UV treated and obviously designed to be in the sun. Along with UV treatment the plastic is also treated with thermal stabilizers. The reinforced layer is made of scrim which is a strong rough fiber that is often used in manufacturing. The scrim layer is laid out in a diamond like pattern that strongly resembles fishing net with small openings. The inner layer is designed to be the blackout layer. It is specially designed to block out light! What a bonus.

This type of light dep tarp only comes in one thickness- 8 mil. So it is relatively light & easier to pull over the frames. Since the plastic is light and easier to pull it is safe to assume that the tarp is less likely to experience undo forces applied to it.

The benefits of using reinforced plastic are durability and resistance to tearing or ripping. Because it is less likely to tear you will have a lot less worry about light leaks when using this type of tarp. With this additional reinforcement it is safe to say that the service life of the plastic is extended.

Cost should always be on your mind when considering your light dep tarp. Will you buy polywoven, plastic film, or reinforced plastic? Basically you need to do a cost analysis of each type of tarp and make your decision from there. The following process should help you make a decision:

Let's consider polywoven tarps first. Polywoven is very durable and should be purchased in the 10 mil to 12 mil range to truly maximize the benefits. Of course, this is probably the most expensive type of light dep tarp to buy. The benefits are: durable, UV resistant, long lasting, resistant to tears and peace of mind that it will work. The cons are: expensive and heavy.

Next up is plastic film. Plastic film is very easy to work with and should be purchased in the 6 mil to 8 mil range to really get the most out of it. This is definitely the least expensive type of light dep tarp to buy. The benefits are: light, easy to use, inexpensive. The cons are: prone to rips and tears, short life span.

Lastly is the reinforced dep tarp. The reinforced tarp is also easy to work with and can currently only be purchased in one thickness- 8 mil. This is almost as expensive as polywoven, without the lifetime durability. The benefits are: light, easy to use, tear resistant, UV resistant, peace of mind. The cons are: expensive.

So there you have it. From there you need to look at how much money you have in your pocket book. If you have a lot, I would recommend the reinforced plastic simply based on the benefits. If on the other hand you are on a tight budget I would recommend getting the plastic film.

Patching your dep tarp is something that is just a fact of life. When you pull plastic over a frame you are going to get tears and rips in your plastic. Sometimes you have to walk on them and sometimes they get snags on some small protrusion that you didn't even know existed. So of course you will have to repair them. You might use tape, stitching or even sandwiching. Yes, sandwiching, at least that is what I call it.

When you use tape to repair your tarp the first thing you need to consider is: is it light proof? Now your traditional duct tape is not at all light proof. Duct tape is too thin and the wrong color all together. I recommend using Gorilla Tape. The black variety seems the best for light proofing. Gorilla tape is extra sticky so it usually remains stuck on. Before applying the tape you want to clean the surface around the hole so the tape will actually adhere to the plastic and not the grime on the plastic!

Stitching is a great technique to use when you have long tears in your dep tarp. All you need is some good string or fishing wire and you stitch the rip up. When you are finished stitching it up I recommend applying a layer of tape just to make sure that you have blocked all the light out.

Sandwiching is when you use two pieces of material, such as plywood, and place them over the tear on either side of the plastic. Then you screw the pieces of plywood together. This is a very effective method of repair! However, I only recommend using this technique for major repairs or if nothing else is available because it makes the tarp very heavy!

Splicing occasionally has to happen. Splicing is the process of combining two pieces of plastic to make a longer or wider tarp. Overlapping and tape are key to this process. I'm sure you are wondering what situation would arise in order for me to splice some plastic together. Well, here are some real life scenarios that I've ran into...

One year I decided to extend the dep by about 20 feet. So I had to make a choice, either buy all new plastic or splice onto the old dep tarp. I decided to splice on a piece of plastic to the old tarp. This is not ideal. The splice WILL fail at some point and it makes using the dep tarp a bit harder, but not extremely hard.

Another scenario that happened was a major rip occurred that was essentially not reparable. Again the choice was buy a new tarp (which can take up to 3 weeks to arrive) or splice. I chose splicing as it was faster and cheaper on the old wallet.

Here is how to splice... The end you are splicing you want to lay it out nice and flat. Next place the new piece evenly and directly on top of the original piece with an overlap of 6 feet to 10 feet. Now we tape it with some good ol' Gorilla Tape. Make sure to clean all the surfaces that are coming into contact with the tape. You will want to tape the ends and the seams where the edges of both plastics meet. This means you will have to flip the tarp over to tape the back side as well. And there you have it, Splicing 101!

Light dep tarps only come in three combinations of color that I'm aware of. They are as follows: black on black, silver on black, or white on black. Let's go over the pros and cons of each one.

Black on black is first up. The pros of black on black are: it usually is a film plastic so it comes in the thickness range of 6 mil to 8 mil. This type of plastic is easily the most affordable and can be bought anywhere. The cons of black on black are: because it is black on black the side facing out is black which will lead to excessive heat inside the covered area. This can have serious detrimental effects on your plants. The tarp usually doesn't last long either.

Next up is the silver on black. The pros of silver on black are: it is usually polywoven and comes in the thickness range of 10 mil to 12 mil. It is very durable and strong with usually a long work life. The silver side is the side that should face out and it reflects the light and reduces the heat tremendously when compared to the black on black tarps. The cons of this type of tarp are: it's heavy to work with, and fairly expensive.

Lastly is the white on black. The pros of white on black are: it is usually plastic film and comes in the thickness range of 6 mil to 8 mil. This means it's light and easy to work with. The white is the side facing out and it does the best job of reducing heat on the inside. The tarp is typically UV treated to extend its service life. The cons of this type are: more expensive than black on black.

Maintenance is where it's at when protecting your investment of a light dep tarp. It really is all about repairing, maintaining, and storing your dep tarp during the season and off season.

We went pretty in depth in how to repair your tarp. You should look over your tarp at least twice a week. It's worth the time and it is done pretty quickly. Well worth the investment of a couple minutes to ensure that your harvest is a successful one.

As for maintenance you basically want to try and keep the dep tarp as clean as possible. I know out in the field this is an impossibility, but you can surely try. Try to minimize the amount that you walk on the plastic itself. You should know that you WILL have to walk on it but plan ahead and keep it on the side that is less likely to be walked on.

During the offseason you want to take that tarp and spread it out completely and let it dry out. This should take a few hours if it's not raining. After it is dry fold it up nice and tight. Now all you need to do is store it in a cool dry place out of the sun. These simple steps will insure that your investment in your dep tarp will last for years to come.

6 HOW TO COVER & UNCOVER YOUR MANUAL DEP

The chapter you have been waiting for! How to cover a giant greenhouse by hand! Now, if you have never covered a light dep you will have some questions on how to do it properly. This chapter is designed to help you answer those questions and hopefully help you to develop techniques to get the job done properly.

First off, to cover a light dep is not hard, in theory. Sometimes in the real world it can be hard as hell. So where to start? You will want to start out at one end of the frame and pull the plastic up and over the frame. This can be easy or it can be hard.

Pulling the plastic over the frame will be fairly easy if you can easily reach the peak of the frame. If, on the other hand, you can't reach the top of the frame you are going to have some problems.

So you got the plastic over the frame at one end- now what? You will want to keep pulling the plastic over the frame as you slowly walk to the other end. This means every couple of feet you will grab the plastic that you can reach and pull it down some more.

You will not be able to pull the plastic all the way down to the ground at first. Once you have pulled the plastic halfway over the frame and halfway down the length of the frame stop what you are doing and go to the other end. The end that you haven't pulled down yet.

Now grab this end and pull it over the frame. This side should go over nice and easy because a lot of the weight has already been lifted over the frame by your initial first pulling.

Once you have this end over the frame you need to try to pull it to the ground. If you can, great. If you can't then just keep walking down and pulling it as much as you can. You may need to make several passes walking along the frame and pulling the plastic until it is fully over the frame and some excess is on the ground.

The first few times you do this are somewhat challenging, but as you go along you should be able to develop a strategy that makes the job easier and faster.

So you have successfully pulled the plastic over the frame. Now it is time to deal with the ends. To correctly set the ends you will need to grab the very center of the plastic on the ends at the ground. You know that piece of plastic that is located dead center of the frame end and is touching the ground.

Once you have found this spot you need to grab it and pull it away from the end of the frame. This is just to remove any excess plastic that may be sagging in the middle. Do not, I repeat do not, yank the plastic as hard as you can because you may inadvertently shift the entire dep tarp! You only want to use enough force to remove the wrinkles.

Now that you are holding the plastic and have removed the wrinkles you want to walk that plastic to one side of the end cap. It does not matter which side you choose to walk it to. After you have walked it one side you will be able to easy lay it down and put a weight on it. The reason you did this whole procedure with the end is to make it easy to weight the plastic down in a secure manner that is also lightproof. If you just bunch it up and put a weight on it you have a good chance of causing a light leak or two. My good friend and world renowned grower buddy, Kevin Jodrey, taught me this technique. It works great. Use it. You will of course want to do both ends!

Let's get back to the whole getting your plastic over the peak. Like I said, if you can reach the peak of your frame you will be fine. However, if you are short, like me, you get to deal with the pain in the ass problem of getting the plastic over the peak of the frame.

I will not lie this can be very difficult if you just try to pull it over the frame. Us shorter folk need to develop strategies and techniques to simplify the job at hand. Here are a few that I have used in the past:

If your frame is made of PVC it is very flexible. I have just grabbed the peak and pulled it downwards. While holding it down I have pulled the plastic over the frame. This technique works pretty well but it does take a certain amount of strength and agility.

I have placed a step stool at the end of the light dep and used this to pull the plastic over. This can be a little dangerous if you step up too high on the stepstool. Make sure that the stepstool is stable and don't yank the plastic real hard. Instead try to apply steady pulling force to get the plastic over the peak.

One of the easiest techniques that I have used is to create a hand tool that is made out of PVC. All it is a length of PVC that is 2 to 3 feet in length. On the end I put a tee coupler to blunt the end so it wouldn't rip the plastic. You could really use anything to blunt the end. A rag and some duct tape would work perfect. So what I did with the tool was put it under the plastic as I was pulling it over the frame. This extended my "reach" and allowed me to easily push the plastic over the top of the frame.

This one technique made my job dramatically easier and cut off 15 to 20 minutes of work every time I had to pull the plastic over the frames. When using this technique you really should use PVC because it is lightweight and fits nicely into your hand. Also you can make a tool for each end super fast and easy.

Sometimes you are just going to need to yank the hell out of that plastic. When you yank the plastic it really does start to hurt your hands. I really noticed that it would start to push my fingernails back into my fingers. Let me tell that shit starts to ache rather quickly.

A great way to deal with that is to make a handle. When you have a handle it is fairly easy to yank on the plastic because you will be able to comfortably apply more force. And since you will be able to apply more force you won't have to yank as much. You will instead be able to just pull the plastic over.

The best way to locate a handle is to find the key positions. There are usually three key positions when you are placing a handle. They are at both ends and at the dead center along the length of the light dep plastic.

Now that you have you locations it is time to make a handle. To make a handle you are going to need a small rock the size of a golf ball or a golf ball and some rope. You will want the rope to be thick enough that is doesn't dig into your hand. Paracord is far too skinny. But if that is all you have you can use it and tie it to a piece of wood or PVC for a handle.

What you want to do is grab the edge of the plastic that you will be pulling to get the tarp over the frame. Make sure that you are at one of the three key positions. Now place the rock on the underside of the plastic that will be exposed when the plastic is pulled over the frame. You know the side of the plastic that is on the inside of the frame? That is the side where the rock should be located. If you are using black and white plastic you want the rock on the black side.

Now go to the white side of the plastic and bunch the plastic up around the rock. You will want to make sure that the rock is close to the edge but not right on top of it. 6 to 10 inches from the edge of the plastic should do it. Now that you have your rock all bunched up in the plastic it is time to tie it up.

To tie it up you need to wrap the rope around the base of the plastic and rock. Make a few loops that are super tight and then start to make knots. I tend to make far more knots then I need. You can choose how many you want and need. Just make sure that it is not coming undone.

How long should you make the handle? At the end locations you only need the rope length of the handle to be a foot long or so. At the center location you will need it be much longer because you may walk through the canopy. Your handle will have to stretch all the way over the frame when the plastic is in the open position. This means that your rope length may be 15 to 20 feet long. You will also want to tie the loose end of the center handle to something stationary because you don't want it to go flying back over the frame when you uncover the frame. Just make sure that your length is long enough that the plastic can go all the way back in the open position.

The great thing about making a good handle is it disperses the force over a larger area of plastic. What this means to you is it doesn't tend to damage the plastic when you are applying a strong force. Unlike yanking the plastic by hand- which is a much smaller area then the handle technique.

Leverage is really what you are looking for- the easiest and best way to impart force so that you are getting the job done without harming yourself and without harming the plastic. Every situation and scene is going to be different. You just need to assess where to find the best leverage. If you are doing light dep in a greenhouse you may end up attaching a pulley to the greenhouse and tying a rope to plastic. I've done that- it works great. As you spend more time pulling you will figure out what works best to get the plastic over the frame.

Once you have the plastic pulled over the frames you will need to secure it down. The most common method to secure the plastic is to use some type of weights or clamps. Your weights can be anything that is heavy and long. Long helps a lot because it covers a longer area. To secure the plastic down I have used pipes, 2x4's, tires, plywood, 5 gallon buckets and branches. Pretty much anything that has some weight to it will work.

Clamps work really well too. You just clamp the plastic to the base of the ribs. I still feel that you may want to use something to weight down the plastic because of the wind.

The only reason we are weighting down the plastic is because of the wind. If there wasn't any wind we wouldn't need to weight it down. Without wind the plastic would just lay there all nice and pretty. But that ain't reality.

Depending on your location wind can be really fierce or not much of a problem at all. Almost everywhere I have seen a light dep wind is a real issue. This is why you need to secure it down. When the wind is blowing all it needs is that one little opening and it can completely rip the plastic off the whole frame in a heartbeat.

Basically, if the wind gets a hold of your dep tarp you will have a giant sail whipping around. And if the wind is really fierce good luck getting that tarp back in place let alone under control. The wind can also turn a little rip into a giant tear if you are unlucky. So keep your tarps in good repair and weight them down properly.

Covering a greenhouse is very similar to covering a frame and yet it is so much harder to do. There is not much friction between a frame and the dep tarp unlike a greenhouse and dep tarp. The reason it is so much harder to cover a greenhouse is because of the additional friction between the greenhouse plastic and the light dep plastic. Instead of having a few points of contact with a frame you now have contact at virtually every point on the surface of the greenhouse. Because of this additional friction you will need to pull the plastic that much harder.

My recommendation is to use small greenhouse frames to make the job easier. Don't fool yourself into thinking that you are going to cover a big greenhouse easily. I have done that in the past. It was a bitch. You know what I used to cover it? A 4 wheeler! I pulled the giant ass dep tarp over the greenhouse with a 4 wheeler. Talk about a bitch. If you plan to cover a big greenhouse make sure you have a very durable dep tarp and a lot of power to pull it over.

If for some reason it rains when you are covering a greenhouse you need to know that the friction force increases by at least double. Hell, when the greenhouse got wet it really felt like it was 5 times harder!

I know I haven't gone over how to uncover. It is so simple. You just pull the plastic back. Start at one end and then go to the other end and pull it back. The plastic will practically fall back by itself. It is much easier to do then covering. You got this.

You may have heard of arms for pulling tarps. An arm is a device that is used on the ends of the frames that helps to pull the plastic over the frame. First of all they do work, but they only really work on shorter frames. Once the arm gets over 7 feet in height it becomes a real bitch to get it over the frame. So if your frame is 8 feet or less you can try out an arm. It may just work out for you. They are easy to make with some pipe. Just look up a picture online if you want to make one. You will need to secure it to the ground. I mean very secure because there is a lot of force that will be applied to the arm!

7 AUTOMATIC LIGHT DEP

Everyone who has ever done light dep has had the thought, "What if I could automate this?" Well, automatic light dep is real and here to stay. An automatic light dep is a device created to automatically cover your light dep at certain times of the day. There are several commercial varieties to choose from but they have similar things in common. They are electrically based, have motors, a power source and a timer.

I have seen some homemade versions that were pretty ingenious. Unfortunately, none of them were viable for commercial use. They were all far too elaborate and depended on the natural resources of each location. My favorite one was powered by water and and a water timer. When the water timer opened, the water would fill a hanging 50 gallon drum which would in turn close the light dep. When it was time to open the light dep another timer was used to empty the 50 gallon drum. It was a tinkerers dream! Boy I loved watching that gadget work!

I too had the dream of an automatic light dep device. I pursued it halfheartedly for years. The more I thought about it the more I wanted one! The thought process was a self feeding vicious circle. The more I tried to create one the more I wanted one! Eventually through a series of fortunate/unfortunate events I actually created one! Let me tell you that having one of these bad boys is a serious game changer. It worked so great I actually decided to sell them! Check them out at humboldtlightdep.com

All commercial light dep devices run on similar principles. They have a motor that "opens" and "closes" the light dep at given times. From there each can vary widely. I have seen some that cover an entire big greenhouse. I have seen some that work inside a greenhouse and use curtains to cover the light dep. Hell, I have even seen one type where they cut off the roof of a shipping container and have that open and close at certain times. They all work and depending on your budget and needs the right one is out there for you.

I am sure you are wondering how reliable they are. And you should be wondering that because your whole future is depending on it. Well, the answer is they are very reliable. The devices are based on old technologies that have been repurposed for light dep. We are talking about electrical motors and timers. How reliable are those in your experience? In my experience they are ultra reliable. In fact 99.9% of the time that one of those devices has "failed" on me was due to my error. As we like to say in the working world "operator error".

If you have ever grown indoors you depended on your timer to turn your lights on and off. There is no difference with an auto light dep. It is the exact same principle. Timer clicks on and the light dep opens up. The timer clicks off and the light dep closes. Nothing new there.

All I'm saying is you can count on the auto light deps to work.

Most auto light deps are designed to work on or off grid. If they are designed to work on grid you just plug it in after you set it up and then you set the timer and you are good to go. The only thing you have to worry about is power failure. If and when you are a victim of power failure all you need to do is reset the timer if it is mechanical or do nothing if the timer is digital. I personally trust mechanical timers more than I do digital timers. This is not to say I don't use digital timers. I absolutely do use digital timers. I am just saying if I had to pick between the two I would choose a mechanical timer because it would be harder to "fry" the timer if there was a power surge.

Now if your light dep is in the boonies (as in off grid) then you will be happy to note that you can still use an auto light dep because, as I said, most are able to function off grid. To power an off grid auto light dep you will need some car batteries to power the timer and motors. You will also need to create a recharging station for the batteries. There are several ways to recharge your batteries. Here are a few options available to you: you can use solar panels to recharge the batteries with or without a charge controller (a charge controller is a device that is used to protect your battery from overcharging). You could use a generator and a battery charger to recharge your batteries. Lastly you could have two sets of batteries that you exchange out and recharge them at a later time and place. All the methods mentioned will work great. In my opinion the best method is using a solar panel with a charge controller. This allows your batteries to be recharged everyday without overcharging your batteries. For less than $300 you can set a panel and a charge controller yourself and be done with it. If you don't have any experience with solar panels and batteries I urge you to do your research before you decide to hook them up!

The best part of using an automatic light dep is how much money it will save and make you. I am sure you are wondering how both of those things are possible at the same time. Fortunately for you those two concepts are not mutually exclusive. You will be able to save money on wear and tear, labor, and time.

Using an auto light dep will make your dep tarps last longer. This is because the auto light deps are not designed to use brute force to get the plastic to cover the light dep. The devices are designed to use a method that is efficient and easy because the motors that they use would not be able to last long if it had to use brute force. This means that your dep plastic will not be yanked up and over your frames. Instead there will be a smooth and repeatable path that is used every time the dep is opened and closed. With an efficient method to cover your dep, your dep tarps will last longer before you are required to replace them.

Because an auto light dep device covers and uncovers your dep for you, you will no longer need to hire someone to cover and uncover your light dep every day. This does not mean that you will not need day labor help. Day labor help is someone you hire by the day to do certain tasks that you need help with. Such as pruning, transplanting, and harvesting. If you needed help with these tasks before you will still need help with these tasks after getting an auto light dep. That is not going to change. However, your helper is not going to need to be there 5 days a week to pull tarp unless you want him there 5 days a week for some other reason.

Talk about a massive savings! Suddenly you are cutting your labor costs in half or more! That is huge. If you feel bad because you feel like you are taking away a job from someone who needs it keep this in mind: With the money that you save you will be able to expand (like you've probably always wanted but couldn't afford to). Well, now you can afford the expansion and with that expansion comes more work. So you will be able to hire them on full time again.

An auto light dep gives you the capacity to make the most of your labor. Instead of paying someone to waste their time on pulling plastic to cover and uncover the dep, you will pay them to do something far more important. Which is to take care of the plants! Can you imagine how much more you will be able to produce because your employee's sole job is to take care of the plants 8 hours a day? Now they will have time to water, spray, prune, plant, transplant, fertilize and do general maintenance every day, all day! With this kind of attention your plants should not only look great, they should be bigger and better than ever. Why? Because if your plants are given the attention that they need from the beginning they will grow at an optimal rate the whole season. This means that they will bigger and healthier sooner than they have ever been before. Bigger and healthier plants do produce bigger bud and better yields!

If you get an auto light dep you will also be able to save on YOUR time. Instead of wasting your time pulling a tarp or being on-call to pull the tarp you will be able to do other tasks. We all know that pulling tarp takes about 15 to 20 minutes each time. This does not include the time you have to take out of your day to be at the dep location to do it. If you are lucky you live on the same piece of property as the dep it is not such a big deal. If you are unlucky and you don't live on the property with the dep this means you may have to commute more than two hours away. Think of all the opportunity costs lost there.

Basically, with a manual light dep you are tied to the dep location and can't get away until the job is done. AND we are talking everyday! How much would it be worth to you to be able to get those thousands of hours back? How much would it be worth to you to be able to spend that time doing stuff far more important to you? You could be spending that time with your family, your friends, your kids, or even spend it going to a concert (like I do!). The time you save not having to pull the tarp will give you the freedom you need to network and relax. If you are like me these things are imperative to your sanity! Why do you think I invented an auto light dep? It was for my sanity!

To get peak light for your crop with an auto light dep system is literally as easy as setting a timer. All you need to do is figure out when the best times of the day are for your plants and you just have to go to your timer and set that in there. No muss no fuss. And now your plants are getting the absolute best possible solar window which means you'll be getting the absolute best possible bud! And because you are getting the highest intensity light your plants will grow to their full potential for their location. That means you will be fully maximizing your location and yield. All with the push of a button!

You will also be able to uncover your plants at night hassle free by setting the timer. If you recall uncovering your plants at night prevents the moisture from building up too much when your plants are in flower. So you can have your plants covered at 7pm, uncovered at 10pm to reduce moisture, covered again at 5am and uncovered at 7am. All this is done just by setting the timer.

You will literally be able to control the plant's environment to a huge degree. Imagine in the spring when there are cold nights. You can go ahead and leave the auto dep closed to trap in additional heat and have it open in the morning when there is light. You can even run lights at night for light breaking without fear of light polluting the neighborhood. If you are super ambitious you could turn one of these into an indoor grow for the winter at the fraction of the cost of building a building- but that is a different book entirely. The applications are many and lucrative to boot.

Payback time for an auto light dep greenhouse depends a lot on the company and model you choose. If you shop smart your payback time will only be one run. Yes, you heard that right. If you shop smart your payback time will be one run and you'll still make money. You really do owe it to yourself to get one of these bad boys because of all the additional opportunities you will get because you own one.

Of course if you buy one of the expensive ones, it will take longer for the payback time. Probably 2 to 3 runs depending on how big your structure is and how well you do. My question is do you really want to spend all that extra money for the bells and whistles or would you rather just have one that costs less, is rugged, dependable and works? I always choose the one that costs less as long as it is dependable and so should you. You ain't gonna win any prizes for those bells and whistles.

Because an auto light dep greenhouse is so dependable you will be able to avoid a lot of potential hassles with employees. You will be able avoid the drama of scheduling to such a large degree that when you absolutely require them to be at work they should give you no drama whatsoever. How could they? All you will need from them is to show up to do maintenance and check things out. The rest of the time they can spend as they like. If they have a hot date, no problem. They got a concert? No problem. A party? No problem. So when you say I need you here this on date there should be no argument. These machines really are game changers!

For the money that you invest in getting an auto light dep machine you really do get a great return on investment. Within three months of owning one you will have paid yourself back your initial investment. The rest after that is gravy! And your gravy train will last for years to come as long as you take care of it!

If you are serious about getting an auto light dep greenhouse, or retro fitting an existing greenhouse, should visit my website and get informed. Stop by at humboldtlightdep.com

8 TIMING OF DEP COVERING & UNCOVERING

The key factor of successful light dep: when do you open & close the dep? The best time of day to cover is entirely up to you and the conditions you are facing. There is of course an ideal best time to cover for each location. The ideal time to cover is when the plants are getting shaded out.

Now is the *ideal* time to cover the *best* time to cover? Not necessarily. In fact, most times it is not. Why? Because of the conditions of your location and the reality of inconvenience.

I know that may sound baffling so I will clarify. To clarify I will use an example. Let's say that the ideal sunlight exposure is 7am to 7pm. This means you should cover at 7pm and uncover at 7am. Well how realistic is it that you will get up at 6:30am to uncover at 7am? You say you can do that? Well, what if I say that when your buds are getting fat that they can't be covered that long because they will mold? That you will have to uncover them at 10pm and then get up at 4:30am to cover them again so they don't get exposed to the morning light and then you have to get up again at 6:30am to uncover at 7am. Could you or your helpers do that, 60 days straight? Probably not.

What if the best light is from 6am to 8pm? What window should you choose? If you are really motivated then the best window to cover would be from 8am to 8pm. Why? Because your plants won't get as hot under the plastic in the morning as they would in the evening from 6pm to 8pm.

What you need to think about is what conditions are your plants going to be in while under the tarp. What will the temperature be? What will the humidity be? How long are you going to keep them covered?

You need to find the window that is best for your plants but you also need to find a window that you will actually follow. If the best window is from 8am to 8pm but you or your help won't actually consistently cover the dep then that is NOT the best window. The best window is the one you will actually follow through on.

A great default window that a lot of light deppers use is cover at 6pm and uncover at 10pm. This method works really well and is a great general purpose time period. The time window will produce nice giant sticky bud and is probably the most convenient when pulling by hand.

9 WHEN IS THE RIGHT TIME TO BEGIN DEPPING

There are so many little things that you need to consider when deciding on the answer to this question. The first and foremost thing to consider is: how well do you know the variety you are working with?

If you know your variety inside and out this question becomes a whole lot easier to answer. You will know exactly how much it will stretch and grow when you start flowering. You will know exactly when it is going to stop stretching. With this knowledge you will be able to determine if your plants will fill in the canopy completely or if you'll be coming up short.

Once you know your variety you will know if it will produce more bud if it is closely packed in together or if it prefers to have a little space. I can't stress enough that knowing what your variety is going to do will take you to the yield you want.

This means learning as much as you can about your variety before you run with it. Go ahead and read literature on it. These are the important questions you need to find the answers to: How many weeks to finish flower? How much does it stretch into flower? Are there any special nutrient needs? Is it prone to any diseases? What is the average yield per area?

With these questions answered you are far more likely to achieve what you set out to do. You will also be able to determine if your initial goals were unrealistic or whether you are within the range of possibility.

Before you start covering you must have the right plant density. Period. End of story. Otherwise you are just wasting your time. This goes back to knowing your variety. If you know how much they will stretch you will be able to predict when your canopy will be full.

If, on the other hand, you don't know your variety and you have no idea how much they will stretch I have a couple of rules of thumb for you:

-If you know it is an 8 weeker it is safe to assume that they will stretch about an additional 50% of their size before you start covering.

-If you know it is a 10 weeker it is safe to assume that they will double in size when you start covering.

If you don't know how long it will take to flower then here are a couple of things to consider:

-If it has long skinny leaves it is probably a 10 weeker.

- If it has fat leaves it is probably an 8 weeker.

Now that is just a rule of thumb that has many exceptions so the rule that you should use is this: If you don't know anything about the variety you are running then you should let them grow so that the plants are just about touching before you start pulling tarp.

Worst case scenario with this method is your plants are too big. This is nothing a pruning session can't cure when preflower ends.

If you do let your canopy get too big before you start pulling your tarp you will need to prune it back. Especially the tops. I know that sounds bad and it can be. The way to avoid the problems associated with pruning the tops back is to wait. After you prune the tops back you need to wait at least 3 days before you start pulling tarp. This will allow your plant to shift its energy to the new tops which will allow the plants to grow at full steam ahead.

I know you have a schedule that you would like to pull off. Don't let that schedule dictate when you start pulling if your canopy isn't ready. There is nothing worse than getting half the yield you were expecting. This has a tendency to be a bit of a soul crusher. Just be patient and wait that extra week or two and let it be a lesson to you.

If you are behind schedule on your plant size make sure you learn from your mistake and do better next time. Your patience will be rewarded with a great harvest. The extra time you take will also allow you to grow your next round a little bit bigger. Then you won't have to wait as long on the next run for your canopy to fill in. Think of it as extra vegetative time for your next run.

Sometimes your canopy looks great, everything is filled in and it feels like it is time to start pulling tarp. Your plants may not be ready to cover because your plant's roots aren't established. You need at least a week for your plants to establish themselves after being transplanted.

Transplanting almost always stresses out your plant. When you take your plant out of its little pot and place it into another container you are going to damage the roots. I know you were very delicate and all that! But you more than likely damaged the micro roots which are so small that you can't even see them. Unless you are some kind of weed whisperer it is better to assume that you did indeed cause some root damage.

What you want to do after transplanting is to give your plants a week or so for the roots to start growing again. Give them the time they need to reestablish their root system. By giving your plants this time you will end up with a better harvest and a better quality of bud.

How can you tell if your plants are established? The answer is when you start seeing new growth on the majority of your plants then you know that your plants are established. It is safe to assume at this point that the roots at least are ready to start flowering.

If you don't give your plants the time to establish themselves then you are essentially cutting off a week of your flowering cycle. Let's say you are running an 8 weeker and you transplant and immediately start pulling tarp. Well, the first week the plants will spend their energy fixing and producing their root system instead of growing leaves. Week 2 to 8 they will resume their normal flowering pattern. So you will have lost a week of flower time. This will result in a smaller yield not to mention your plants won't stretch as much during preflower. So if you were counting on a good stretch during preflower you are screwed because you didn't let your plants get their roots established.

Give your plants at least a week to get established. You will enjoy the results and so will your plants.

Once your plants are established you will want to make sure that everything is set up right. By everything I am referring to your frame, your plastic and your water. Of course you should have already made sure that all of this stuff was set up correctly in the first place.

This is the time to triple check to make sure that everything is in proper order. Make sure that the water is reliable and can reach everywhere it needs to be. If it isn't then you need to go buy some hose and make sure it can reach where you need it to reach.

Make sure that your plastic is the right size. Is it lightproof? It damn well better be! Check to see if it has any holes and repair them if need be. Is it anchored on one side? Do you have weights set up for the other side to secure it down so the wind won't blow it around?

Your frame should be sturdy enough to hold up your plastic. Make sure it is properly anchored and it has at least one purlin.

Once you have everything set up correctly you will need to be able to pull the tarp for 60 to 70 days straight. Not only to cover it but also to uncover it. You will really want to schedule this time out correctly. You don't get the option of "I'll let it slide today and resume my schedule tomorrow". That is how you end up with crappy weed that may be full of seeds from stressing them out and causing them to hermaphrodite.

Can you set aside all the extracurricular activities that you would like to do for 60 to 70 days straight? That is the question you really need to ask yourself. Not only ask yourself but actually commit to. If you do I assure you that it will be worth it. If you don't commit you will fall short of your goals and you will only have yourself to blame.

Now let me be clear: your two month commitment doesn't mean that you have to be the one to cover and uncover it every day. Of course you might just do it yourself. Or you might hire someone to do it for you. Maybe you will do the majority of it and have someone fill in for a couple of days. Or maybe you will have someone cover for the weekends and you cover during the week. Or maybe you will use an automatic light dep greenhouse. Whatever the case may be is unimportant. You just need to make sure that you get it done.

10 LIGHTING

Sun sweet sun! The sun is the best invention since ever! I mean that. Without the sun none of this would be possible and I'm not just talking about growing some sweet ass smoke. The sun is the driving force of life on this planet. So back to my original point which is use the sun as much as you can.

The sun provides us with so much free energy, light and heat that it makes growing three runs a year possible without having to foot a huge electric bill. Besides plants on this planet have adapted over thousands and thousands of years to use the light emitted from the sun. So not only is it free but in all actuality it is the very best light for the plants. Yes even marijuana! All the artificial light that has been created to grow plants are just a pale imitation of the sun and come at a very high cost.

The sunlight on your garden has different intensities throughout the growing year. This is because of the orbit of the earth around the sun and the tilt of the earths' axis. The sun light has to travel through the earth's atmosphere which can be longer or shorter depending on the season. In summer the light from the sun is more intense because the light has to travel a shorter distance through the atmosphere. In the winter the opposite is true. This is why the direct sun light is cooler in the winter- because it has to travel further through the atmosphere to reach the earth's surface.

This is why the location of your structure is so important. The orientation you choose for your structure will affect the overall outcome of yield and quality. When I say orientation I mean are you going to have it run north to south or east to west? That of course means lengthwise. Not only should the orientation of your structure be considered but also your location and potential shading.

When you locate your structure it is very important to remember that the path of the sun moves. What is a great location for sun in the summer may be a shitty location in fall. You need to consider what has the potential to cause shading in the present and the future. Some of the things that cause shading can be dealt with such as trees or brush. But if it is a hill, well, you are better off moving your location because obviously you can't move a hill.

So it is in your best interest to maximize the solar resource of your location. Make sure that you choose wisely because without great sun in the spring and fall your potential yield will be smaller than that of a great year round sunny location.

I've seen friends learn this lesson the hard way, and I truly don't want you to experience their loss, so listen up. In the fall the days get shorter. We all know this, no big deal. But did you know that the days get shorter FAST. How is this important? This is important because if you chose a spot that only gets 5 to 8 hours of direct sunlight in the middle of summer, watch out in the fall. My friends thought: "Oh no problem, my plants will finish before it becomes a problem." Boy were they wrong! The light changed so fast from 8 hours of direct sunlight a day to a scant 3 hours that the plants did not have the time to finish before mold started rotting the plants. So keep in mind that the tide can turn very fast and you will want to plant your varieties according to the solar resource available to them in that location.

One of the best locations to choose is a hill top because it gets early morning light and late evening light. For light dep you don't exactly need all that much sun in the summer but you will need it in spring and fall.

The best way to find out how much sun a location gets year round is using a device called a Solar Pathfinder. The cost of a Solar Pathfinder is about $300. The Solar Pathfinder uses old school technology to accurately determine exactly how many hours of sun any spot will receive year round. The device uses a glass dome, a compass, and a special sheet of paper with columns and rows of information on it. You set the magnetic declination on the device, level it up and presto bingo! you can calculate exactly how many hours of direct sunlight that location will receive.

Peak Light

Let's talk about peak light, what is it, how to achieve it and the benefits. Peak light is the best window of light any location receives during the day. For example, imagine there is a garden that in summer receives 15 hours of sunlight, but only 10 hours of direct sunlight, and the rest of the sunlight is shaded out and indirect. So for that particular garden those 10 hours are considered peak sunlight. The only problem is that those 10 hours of great sunlight occur from 9am to 7pm. This means that in order for the plants to receive the very best sunlight they must be covered at 7pm and uncovered at 7am. This can be very problematic depending on all sorts of factors that are covered in this book. But the most important one is this: Are you willing to get up at 6:45am every day to uncover?

The benefits of using peak light should be obvious. By using the best, most intense light you will get a bigger harvest. What I mean by bigger is more weight. Not only that but your bud will have a higher concentration of THC, the bud will look better than bud harvested in the fall, and your plants will be less susceptible to disease because they will be healthier.

Light Leaks

Now that you have chosen the best solar resource spot and oriented your structure properly it is time to talk about light leaks. Light leaks are exactly what they sound like. When you have your plants covered over with a dep tarp there will almost always be some light that is leaking in. This is bad, but not as bad as others would have you believe. You need the light dep to be dark enough to set your plants to flowering. Well, how dark is that?

Let's start with what we already know to be true. Starlight doesn't negatively affect the budding cycle. Neither does the full moon for that matter. A full moon night is pretty damn bright if you have ever been out in one. So that is what we know for sure.

So when you cover your plants, the inside of the structure should be darker than a full moon night but can be lighter than a starry night. I know that sounds vague but it is actually a great gauge. The plastic itself should be lightproof as in no light gets through. As you use the plastic you will notice tiny holes on the inside. Tiny holes are no problem unless you have a bunch of them, if your tiny holes go from a starry night to full moon night you need to start repairs. Just patch them up as you go with Gorilla tape. And patch up the big holes as well obviously!

Uninterrupted darkness has been achieved! So what? Well when your plants receive 12 hours or more of uninterrupted darkness on a REGULAR schedule they start to flower. I hope you caught that emphasis on *regular* schedule. It is very important that the plants receive a consistent amount of darkness on a regular schedule so that they can perform optimally. Optimally, in this case, is flowering like crazy.

The plants will begin to show signs of flowering within the first week or two depending on the variety. The first signs of flowering are sending out small flowers at the branch internodes and at the tips of each branch including the top of the plant. The plants will continue to stretch up to three weeks and then settle down into serious flowering. This is only possible if you give your plants 12 or more hours of uninterrupted darkness on a regular schedule. Don't dick around with it.

Supplemental lighting

Supplemental lighting should be used in the spring and fall to help you achieve your maximum potential as a gardener. Supplemental lighting is adding artificial light to your garden during the day or night. I know, I said to use the sun as much as possible, and it's true that you should. However, in the spring and fall the sun's intensity on your plants is not enough to achieve the optimal growth that you need. The intensity of the sun is low due to seasonal conditions such as clouds, short days, and the sunlight having a long distance to travel through the atmosphere as explained earlier.

So in order to achieve optimal growth in spring you will need to add light to your plants during the day. I recommend using at least three hours of light on the plants during the day. Three hours seems to keep them going really well in spring. Enough so that they are growing and healthy. How much light should you use? Well that depends on how big of an area you are covering. My rule of thumb for plants outside is this: A 1000 watt HID light will cover about a 10 foot by 10 foot area. You will need to raise the light about 8 to 10 feet off the ground to achieve this spread. A 600 watt light will cover about an 8 foot by 8 foot area when raised 8 to 10 feet off the ground. Remember to only use lights that are rated to be outside or in a greenhouse.

Light Breaking

Growing in spring has other hazards besides low intensity light. Namely flowering. The days are so short that your plants WILL start to flower. If this happens you are done! Kiss all your hard work goodbye because once your plants start to flower it will take at least a month to snap out of it. This means your plant's growth will stop and they will be small and scrawny when you need them to big and healthy.

This is where light breaking comes in. Light breaking is the technique of interrupting the dark cycle with light. I recommend using 1 to 2 hours of light on your plants at night. Some varieties only require a short burst of light while other varieties require more. That is why I recommend 1 to 2 hours. If you want to be on the safe side you should do 2 hours. Now this is important, when you turn on the light it should be sometime between 11pm to 3am. This way your plants won't receive too much uninterrupted darkness. This technique is how to grow your plants big enough so that it is possible to grow three harvests a year. Use it and you will hit the ground running in spring and be ahead of everyone.

Light breaking and adding supplemental light is easy if you have **on grid power**. On grid just means you have a power source from the power company running to your structure. If you have grid power you are on easy street. You will be able to run an extension cord to your structure to power your lights. All you need at this point is a timer and you are set. The hardest thing that you will be doing is making a frame to hang your lights. Go get yourself an all weather light fixture and get started is what I say.

On the other hand, if you are out in the sticks you don't have the luxury of on grid power. Oh well- no use crying over what can't be changed today. So you are **off grid** and need to provide power to lighting system? This is definitely problematic but not impossible. You really have two options. They are using a self start generator that is hooked up to a timer or an alternative energy system. If you have a self start generator then you can run your system like it is hooked to the grid. Have the genny start for 3 hours a day and 2 hours at night. You are good to go!

If you are off grid and on **alternative energy** then this changes everything. You will not be able to provide your plants with supplemental lighting during the day. You will only be able to do light breaking at night. If you are wondering why, the answer is it would be far too expensive to create a system to do both. But if you have enough money you can design anything.

You are going to want to design a system that not only powers your lights but does so in a sustainable manner. You will have to design a lighting system that takes these basic criteria into account. How big of an area are you covering? How intense do you want the light to be? How long do you want the lights to run? How long do you want the system to be autonomous? Are you going to use 12Vdc or 24Vdc?

Once you have answered these basic questions you can get down to designing your system. Your system should be able to cover the area of your plants with sufficient light that they do not go into flowering. It is always better to err on the side of caution and give them too much light rather than not enough. In an off grid situation I would recommend a 1 to 1.5 hour light schedule to save on power. As for the autonomy of your system I would recommend at least 5 days. This means that your system can run at least 5 days on its own without interruption. Choose whatever voltage you want. I usually choose based on the availability and prices of the lights and timers.

You can achieve all this through the use of solar panels, batteries, a charger, lights, light fixtures (an extension cord with light bulb outlets on it), a timer and a generator. That is the entire list! Seriously that's all. You could use a solar charge controller to protect your batteries, but that is up to you. Most of this stuff can be purchased on Amazon for a very reasonable price. I would definitely buy your light bulbs, timer, solar panels and light fixtures on Amazon. They will ship it to you and you'll most likely get a better price than you would at the store.

The system works like this. The solar panels charge the batteries during the day. The batteries supply the power for the lights which is in turn regulated by a DC powered timer. The generator is used to recharge the batteries once every five days if the solar panel is not able to recharge the batteries fast enough. That is the system in a nut shell.

Designing the system is beyond the scope of this book. If you don't feel confident in designing one there are many alternative energy companies out there that will design one for you. Don't buy anything from them as they will charge you an arm and a leg. Instead have them design the system and you go buy what you need on your own.

I can help you choose your lights though. The two basic options for off grid lighting are Compact Florescent Lights (CFL) and Light Emitting Diode (LED). They are both outstanding devices and use far less electricity than an incandescent light bulb or a High Intensity Discharge (HID) bulb.

Lets start with the **CFLs**. The CFL will give you approximately 45 Lumens per Watt which is a good return on electricity investment when compared to an incandescent bulb. A CFL does put out a good amount of light and it is not directional, so you will get a better spread of light to cover the given area. When the CFL emits light it emits light in all the directions that the bulb itself is facing. This means it emits light up as well as down. The light going up is essentially being wasted because there are no plants up there. CFLs run a little warm which is wasted energy. Another thing to consider is the temperature and how the temperature affects a CFL. If the temperature is too cold the CFL will be dim when it is on. If it is really cold, such as 20 degrees Fahrenheit or below, the CFL will not "ignite" and won't turn on. So if you are in a cold climate or experience cold a part of the year you should not use a CFL.

Now let's talk about **LEDs**. The LED will give you approximately 100 Lumens per Watt. Currently this is the best use of electricity in the lighting world. However, the LED is very directional. Meaning the bulbs only will give off light in one direction unless there is a diffuser on the bulb. Make sure to buy bulbs with diffusers! Other than that drawback they are the best bang for your buck. They don't have temperature threshold problems. Meaning they will turn on even if it is super cold.

For both types of lights you will want to protect them from the elements unless otherwise stated by the manufacturer.

As the seasons change it is important to remember that the available solar light resource changes as well. From month to month the availability, intensity, and heat from the sun will change. You need to keep track of these parameters. If your plants aren't getting enough light during the vegetative or flowering stages you will not be happy with the results. If your plants aren't getting enough intense light you will not be happy with the results. If your plants aren't getting enough heat from the sun you will not be happy with the results. Are you sensing a theme here? GOOD.

Fortunately for you all of these things you can control by artificial means. If you pay attention and keep track of what is happening with your plants you will be able counteract 99% of what nature throws at you. But only if you pay attention.

11 STRAINS

Time is of the essence when you are going to plan a run (or three!). Before you choose the variety that you want to run in your light dep you need to decide whether you are going to start from seed or clone. Each has their own benefits and drawbacks, such as uniformity, finish time and speed at which they finish.

Seeds are such a wonderful resource. They pack so much in such a little package. With a seed you get some seriously fast growth because of the hormones they release as they sprout. But there are drawbacks. They take a lot longer to get to proper size for depping because they start out so tiny. There is always the possibility of the dreaded male which should be avoided at all costs (especially if you are inexperienced with males). With seeds it is impossible to achieve relative uniformity because they are all different genetically from each other. If you have a stable line then you will get a fairly uniform outcome but you have to remember you are dealing with different phenotypes (brothers and sisters) so there will be genetic variation. With that variation you may have different looks, growth rates, and different times at which they should be harvested.

Clones on the other hand should be "knowns". You should know what the plant will look like, smell like, taste like, and how many weeks it takes in flower before it is ready to harvest. This is because a clone from the same mother is the same plant. NOT similar. It is exactly the same plant with the exact same DNA.

When you light dep you really should use clones because you will be able to get uniform growth, and be able to harvest at the same time, which will save you tons of work in the long run. I am not saying don't experiment a little. Of course you should, have a little controlled fun. You'll learn something and maybe even be able to use the knowledge for personal gain.

So now that I have convinced you to start with clones (right?) it is time to choose the type of strains that you want to grow. So let's start with some basic information first. There are two main types of marijuana plants: sativa and indica. Let's be clear, there are almost no pure strains of sativa or indica out there. You may hear someone talk about it like it is the holy grail of weed. It's not. Genetic breeding has become so good that true sativas and indicas are basically a novelty at this point. They are really only good for breeding characteristics into other plants. This is not a breeding book sooo....

Sativa is native to the tropic regions and has developed characteristics to deal with that environment. The plant is known for being lanky or long. It will keep growing and stretching to reach the light. The roots like lots of room to grow and the plant doesn't like high concentrations of fertilizer. The flowering time for a sativa is long. Anywhere from 10 to 16 weeks. This is because in the tropics the plant doesn't experience a true winter so it is able to keep on growing with impunity. The buds tend to be slightly airy and the high from smoking it is considered to be soaring.

Indica is native to the high elevation of the Kush Mountains and it has adapted to that particular environment. The plant is known for being squat with big leaves. I mean BIG when they are in full growth. The roots of the plant do not need lots of room because there is not a lot of native soil high in the mountains where they developed. However their Native Kush Mountains are known for their naturally higher concentrations of minerals. This means that indicas tend to be heavy feeders. The flowering time for an indica is approximately 8 weeks or less. This is because the weather turns fast in the mountains. One day it is summer and the next it is like winter and the plant knows this so it finishes fast! The buds tend to be super dense and sticky. The high from smoking this type of weed is stupefying as in couch lock.

Those are the basics of the two types of main strains out there.

99.9% of the strains out there and available to you are hybrids of those two types of plants. This is great for you because you don't have to spend years breeding plants to develop the exact strain you want. Someone has already done it and all you have to do is decide which one you want.

When considering the strain or strains you want to grow you must consider the potential THC/CBD production of the plants you grow. Now, most strains out there have a known range of THC/CBD that they can produce. The reason that a strain has a range of THC/CBD and not a constant number is simple. The way you grow your plant has a major impact on the THC/CBD production of the plant.

Tetrahydrocannabinol (THC)- say that fast five times! I'm sure you know what it is but if you don't: THC is the psychoactive chemical in marijuana. It's the shit that gets you high! Can't believe I finally got to write that in a book! Sorry.

For example let say you are growing Blue Dream with a THC range of 17% to 24%. Now you are kicking ass and your Blue Dreams are receiving the optimal growing conditions. So their THC production was maxed out at 24%. Now let's say Joe Blow grew the exact same clones as you and his THC production was 18%. Why? Because he constantly underfed and under watered them. He also didn't locate them properly so they didn't receive the best light. All of these things matter for your THC production. Don't forget it.

Cannabidiol (CBD) is a non psychoactive chemical also found in marijuana and it has a lot of beneficial medical uses. THC helps with pain relief, nausea control, or anxiety relief. But let's talk about CBD and its benefits for a minute. CBD, much like THC, has a percentage range for each strain. The percentage of CBD is also dependent on the growing conditions as well. The better you treat your plants the higher percentage of CBD. Simple as that.

CBD has a wide range of medical benefits and is currently being studied today. This means more and more benefits will likely be discovered. Here are a few conditions that CBD is known to treat: antiemetic, anticonvulsant, antipsychotic, anti-inflammatory, anti-oxidant, anti-cancer and antidepressant. The list goes on.

Which strain is the best medicine for you? That depends on what kind of ailment you have. I suggest that you do a little research on the internet to figure out exactly what kind of medicine you need. Take the time and get it right.

Have you seen some of the documentaries done on the benefits of CBD? If not you should. Those documentaries are some powerful testimonials of how ridiculous our laws are and how powerful marijuana is as a medicine. Needless to say some of them are touching and emotionally powerful. Watch one or two.

If you are in the market to grow some good CBD plants for medicine, make sure to do your research to find the right strain for you. You may have to do a little more work finding what you want but I promise it is out there and you can find it.

When choosing your strain you will need to consider how long the strain you choose will take to flower. So how long does it take marijuana to flower? It takes approximately 8 to 10 weeks for marijuana to flower. Yes, there are some strains that finish faster and some that finish longer. We are not going to cover those because there are not many of them and if you decide to go with one of those outliers the principles you learn in this book will still apply.

Eight weeks strains, as you can imagine, get this characteristic from their indica side. These plants generally tend to grow a little slower in the vegetative state than their sativa counterpart. This means that when you are growing them up you will want them a little bigger than a 10 week strain before you turn them down to flower. This is because 8 week strains react FAST to the light change. They don't stretch much before they start really producing flowers. This is why you want to grow them a bit bigger.

The great thing about an 8 week strain is the quick turnaround time. You can transplant, cover, and harvest in 9 weeks or less. The 8 week strain finishes fast enough that you are sometimes able to ignore potential problems because the plants can finish before the problem becomes catastrophic.

10 week strains get this particular characteristic from their sativa side. These plants generally tend to grow fast during the vegetative state. They really reach for the light. When it is time to turn down the plants to flower you usually end up turning them down when they seem a little small (depending on planting density of course). This is because the plants will continue to grow and stretch for the first three weeks of flowering. That is why you can turn the lights down when they are a bit smaller because they will grow and fill in the space.

Now with 10 week strains it is very important to monitor potential problems because they are going to be in the ground for 10 weeks so there is no out growing the problem. These plants are slow finishers and to protect them properly all potential problems need to be nipped in the bud.

A thing to consider when choosing an 8 week or 10 week strain is how many harvests are you after? If you are after one or two you can run any strain that your little heart desires. On the other hand if you want to pull three GOOD harvests you have two choices. You can do three runs of an 8 week strain. You can also do three runs with two runs of an 8 week strain and one run with a 10 week strain (hope that made sense). Otherwise you risk one run with subpar light and a bad production. We don't want that.

Some strains have a better potential of yield than other strains. There are high yield strains and low yield strains.

High yield strains tend to be all over the map, they don't fall into one category. Some examples of a high yield strains are Blue Dream, Green Crack, Sour Diesel and of course the infamous Trainwreck. High yield strains can yield up to approximately 1 pound per square yard. That's 1 pound per 3 foot by 3 foot. That is pretty damn good. Of course that is the upper limits. You should set your sights on achieving that outcome but don't be disappointed if you can't quite get there. You may be dealing with limiting factors that you are unaware of and that may your maximum potential yield. That doesn't mean you should settle for less. I say keep trying and keep achieving! You will never know unless you try.

Of course everyone wants a high yield strain and the good news is that most of the common strains out there are high yield strains. If you want a high yield strain make sure to do a little internet research.

Low yield strains seem to stem from the OG family. Now don't get me wrong there are a high yield OG's out there IF you know how to grow them. Skywalker OG, and San Fernando Valley (SFV) OG are two examples of high yield OG's.

Low yield strains tend to fall into what I call the specialty category. People only grow them because there is something really special about them. I mean who wants to spend all that effort and time growing something that doesn't yield a lot of weed? It must be pretty special if they are going to grow it. And it usually is! Some of the special qualities I have run into are: amazing taste, outstanding aroma, insanely beautiful, high CBD content and a crazy high! Here are a few examples of a low yield strains: Girl Scout Cookies, OG Kush, and Pure Kush.

When you decide if you are going to grow a high or low yield strain just keep in mind who you are growing this for. When you ask yourself that question it will be clear which type to choose.

So you have decided on a high yielder (imagine my surprise). Now you need to choose whether you want to grow a green weed or a sour weed.

Green weed has fruity to piney aroma and is pretty easy to grow. They tend to be fast finishers that give a great yield. Green weed is by far and away the more abundant variety grown out there. This has its disadvantages because when it comes time to get rid of it you generally have to take a lower price. Sometimes it is really difficult to get rid of and you just have to wait around until that right person shows up who wants what you have. Or worse, who will settle for what you have. That is a shitty feeling. Spending weeks and months to produce a superior product only to basically be told "I don't want what you got."

The good news is by using light dep you should harvest long before the peak of harvest in the fall and they'll want exactly what you have! And what you have is some beautiful, sticky, green weed that smells like heaven. This is why you want to do light dep- so you will always be in demand. Not sitting on the corner like some outcast!

Here is a small list of great green weed that kicks ass: Blue Dream, Mr. Nice, Purple Trainwreck, Trainwreck, Bleu Cheese, The Cheese, Green Crack, AK47, White Widow and Cherry Pie just to name a few.

Sour/OG strains are called this because of their soury, musty smell. These strains are considered the premier shit out there. People can't seem to get enough of it. The high from these strains seems a lot more powerful than the green strains. So powerful that after a hit or two I hope you aren't busy for at least four hours 'cause you and the couch are gonna need some time together.

When you grow Sour/OG strains you will be a welcome guest no matter what time of the year it is. People will be dying to get a sample of your weed. Especially if you took the time to grow it right. They want it because that shit is special and everyone knows it.

Here is a small list of Sour/OG strains: San Fernando Valley OG, Fire OG, Sour Diesel, Three Kings, Gorilla Glue, Skywalker OG and Versace OG.

Some strains are hearty and more resilient than others. There are also some strains that are susceptible to problems and they need to be treated like babies. As a grower you need to know as much about the strain that you want to grow as you possibly can because with the right knowledge about your strain comes great yield and great quality. Just because a plant is more susceptible to problems doesn't mean it isn't worth growing.

Hearty strains tend to be vigorous growers that are strong and resistant to problems. This does not mean that they will survive any neglect you throw at them and pull off a great harvest. This is hardly the case. What it does mean is they often have the ability to outgrow a problem. This is not always the case of course. The main characteristic of a hearty strain is its wider range of tolerances for potential trouble. But remember each hearty strain has its own set of strengths.

Most hearty strains are able to resist powdery mildew and mold, which is a potential major problem.

The heartiest strain that I know of is Trainwreck. Somehow that strain is able to produce quality bud in less than ideal conditions on a consistent basis. I have literally seen a Bubba's Gift and a Trainwreck side by side in the same shitty conditions and the Trainwreck yielded more than 5 times the amount of the Bubba's Gift. You just gotta love Trainwreck for that.

Here is a small list of some of the hearty varieties out there: Trainwreck, Blue Dream, AK47, Sour Diesel, Green Crack, and Bleu Cheese.

Susceptible strains are usually prone to a lot of different problems such as: mites, mildew, mold, root rot, fertilizer sensitivity and thrips to name a few. They need to be babied along every step of the way. You need to pay attention to them and at the first sign of a problem you need to go to Def-Con 4 and eradicate any source of the problem. Sometimes this means killing a plant or two to prevent the problem from spreading.

I bet you are wondering why anyone would want to grow such a problem child. People grow it because it produces outstanding product. I don't want to scare you away from growing one of these susceptible strains. The truth is once you learn the ins and outs of any strain you won't run into any real problems because your whole process will be one of preventative maintenance. The key is learning the ins and outs. Once you have the knowledge you are good to go.

If you are a beginner grower I would recommend growing a hearty strain and avoiding the susceptible strains until you have pulled off a few harvests. Once you have expanded your plant knowledge then you can delve into the trickier varieties.

Here is a list of susceptible strains that are available out there: OG Kush, Pure Kush, Bubba's Gift, and Guido.

A quick aside: there are many varieties out there that are finicky and take awhile to master. The main varieties of plants that fall into this category are OG's and Kushes. These are not beginner strains! Feel free to practice with a few of them each run so you can get an understanding of what it really takes to master them.

The last, but not least, thing to consider is exactly how many hours of light does your strain require to stay in the vegetative state? Not all strains are the same. Some strains require a lot of uninterrupted darkness before they will shift into flowering, while others will shift into flowering at the drop of a hat.

Most of your 10 week strains are fairly resistant to flowering right away. If you light break for an hour in the middle of the night you will be just fine. They will continue to grow like gang busters.

Just a few of your 8 week strains require at least 18 to 20 hours of light a day to prevent them from shifting into flower. There is an upside to a plant that shifts into flowering immediately. They do very well in shady spots. They will produce big ass buds even in a shady spot. So keep that in mind.

There are two varieties that I know of that are require a lot of light: Mr. Nice and The Crippler. If you decide to grow these varieties just make sure to give them at least 18 hours of light a day or they will start to flower.

12 WATERING

Water is essential to life on this planet as we know it. Pretty much every life form on the planet is made up of water. Not only is life made up of water but life also requires new sources of water on a fairly regular basis. For plants that are considered annuals (they live their entire life in one year) this is doubly true. Think about it, these types of plants have to sprout from seed and grow, grow, grow, before they flower. They grow so fast because they want to put out as many flowers as possible to ensure the next generation. That is asking a lot of any life form. Well, all this growing requires water and depending on the size of your plant it may be a little or a lot.

For marijuana's happiness and health it requires regular watering for it to complete its lifecycle. Watering seems simple enough. You just water and the rest takes care of itself right? Don't you wish! There are so many potential hazards when watering that you should become a bit informed so you can get a kick ass growth rate through the entire lifecycle. Not just in one stage but all the stages should be your goal.

Over watering. Over watering is a killer. There are two types of over watering that I want to talk about. Saturation over watering (this is the one you know about) and per session over watering (this is just wasteful).

Saturation over watering is the one everyone hears about. When someone says "are you over watering?" this is what they are talking about. This type of over watering occurs because you are saturating the soil (or whatever medium you are using) on a regular basis. The watering occurs so regularly that the medium never has a chance to dry out to allow oxygen in.

Now let me clarify what I mean by "dry out". I know it sounds like I am saying let the soil get dry. This NOT AT ALL WHAT THIS MEANS! It means let your medium go from soaking, saturated wet to moist. Moist means the top layer of soil is wet and when you pick up a handful you can't squeeze any water out of it. When someone says let it dry out this is what they mean. You should never, ever let you medium dry out. This is how you kill, ruin or stunt your plants. Don't ever let your plants get dry! When you let your plants get dry all the micro roots that the plant uses to feed and absorb water dry out and die. This will stunt your growth. When you water after that you plants will have to build the whole micro root structure again. It is a waste of your plants energy.

Over watering per session is wasteful on more than just one level. Over watering per session means that, when you see water flow out of the bottom of the container or bed that you are probably over watering. Basically your soil is saturated and you are still watering. Don't do this, it is wasteful. It is okay to let some water flow out from the bottom but don't keep watering for another minute in that spot.

When you over water like that you run the risk of using up all the water you have stored or running up your water bill. If you are in the sticks and use up your water you are good and fucked if you can't get water delivered. With all the droughts that have been happening it is wise to be conservative with your water. Another risk you run from over watering per session is flushing out your nutrients. You know the stuff your plant eats to grow big and strong? You don't want the nutrients running out the bottom of the container so monitor how much you water.

Signs of over watering are often easy to spot. But sometimes they are subtle and will take a little investigating. The basic signs of over watering are: the soil looks waterlogged all the time, there is algae growth on the top of the soil, or there is no growth in the plant.

When a plant is over watered the plants roots have no access to oxygen which helps them grow. These are not aquatic plants (although they can live in water given the right conditions). So if your soil looks waterlogged on a regular basis (like everyday) then you need to let it dry out and adjust your watering cycle. If you have a green growth of algae on the top of your soil you may be over watering. But if your plants look happy and healthy and growing keep watering the way you do because it is clear your plants love what you are doing.

If your plants are not growing even though you have fed them, watered them, kept them warm, and have given them plenty of light, they just might be getting over watered. Try letting them get a little drier before watering again and see what effect it has on them.

Over watering is occasionally due to your soil or containers. Sometimes you end up with a soil mix and container that doesn't drain. This is a difficult one to pick up on at first, but once you know the signs it is easy to spot. The quick test is this. Pick up the container. If it is heavy it's not draining. Now if the container is too big to pick up, I want you to pierce the bottom on the side. If water runs out when you do this you will need to add several more holes to ensure proper drainage.

Under watering is the exact opposite of over watering. This means you are letting your plants get too dry. And worse than that is letting your plants get too dry on a regular basis. Every time your plants get dry your delicate little micro roots die and now your plant has to regrow them. Bummer for you and bummer for them.

There are many potential causes of under watering. Maybe you are not watering often enough, or maybe you need to water longer per session. When you let soil or any medium dry out too much it is a bitch to rehydrate. Once the soil is too dry it actually repels water! This means you will have to go through and water everything once. Then you'll have to go back and water it again and again and again. It usually takes four smaller waterings in one day to completely rehydrate your soil. Why? Think of your dry soil as a grain of uncooked rice. How long does it take for that grain of rice to absorb BOILING WATER? Anywhere from 20 to 40 minutes for uncooked rice. Now if your rice was already cooked and moist it would only take a couple of minutes to add more water to it. Granted, your soil is far more permeable than a grain of rice but you get my point.

There are signs of under watering. Some are glaring while others are a lot harder to spot. The easiest one to spot is a wilting plant. If your plant is wilting and the soil looks dry, that's because it is! Get out the hose and water that shit! If the top of your soil is constantly dry looking you may be under watering. A quick cure for this is to add a 4 to 6 inch layer of mulch. This will hold in the moisture and give your plants a new zone to grow their roots in.

I recommend using alfalfa or straw. Straw is cheaper, but alfalfa is a fertilizer that is slow release so you get 2 in 1 when you use it as a mulch. Remember that as plants grow, their water needs will grow with them. So as they get older you will have to water them more.

The trickiest sign of under watering to spot is the veiny leaves. I know all marijuana leaves have veins, hear me out. When a plant is under watered on a regular basis the leaves contract in order to minimize the leaf's surface area. They do this to conserve the water that they do have. When the leaves are contracted you will notice on the upper side that the veins on the leaves appear to be sunken in like tiny valleys. On the bottom of the leaf the veins will be popping out. For comparison the leaves on a perfectly watered plant will be all spread out and FLAT. They will look vibrant, succulent and juicy. Not veiny at all with little valleys of veins.

You need to become the weed whisperer to water the correct amount. I am serious. If you want to succeed you need to be able to be a weed whisperer. Not THE weed whisperer just a weed whisperer among many. All it takes is practice and paying attention to what the hell you are doing and what the hell the plants are doing. You need to treat each plant as an individual and water that plant accordingly. Just because that plant over there required 30 seconds of water doesn't mean this plant over here will require that much. Just keep your eyes open and pay attention. You will be able to learn all you need to know as you go.

If you want to know exactly how much to water your plants I will tell you exactly how much you should water no matter what the size. You ready? You need to water exactly enough. That's the secret. What is enough? Well each plant is different and has different requirements and you need to learn them.

The way to figure out exactly how much water your plants need is to treat them all the same. Well, in the beginning at least. The best way to do this is to water a plant and count as you water. When you felt like you have watered enough for that plant you stop and remember how high you counted up to. Let's say you counted up to 10 seconds. Now you go to the next plant and water it to the count of 10. Go ahead and water every plant that way.

The next time you water do the same thing and make sure you are paying attention to your plants. Keep doing this until you notice that this plant doesn't need quite a 10 count, maybe it needs an 8 count and that plant over there needs a 13 count because it always looks thirsty.

That is how you develop your watering pattern. Keep in mind that your water pattern should change over time as the plant's water needs change. If you are not changing your count as time goes on you may need to make a change. Just pay attention and everything will be fine.

Morning is the best time of day to water. Especially if you are doing light dep, because you want the water to fully absorb down into the soil. Why? Because when you cover the plants there will be a lot of condensation from the plants releasing water and the soil releasing water. You want to minimize how much water the soil releases while it is covered with plastic. The best way to do this is to water in the morning. What time in the morning? Well, I'll let you figure that out.

When you water in the morning you are also giving your plants the fuel that they need to face the day. It is also a great way to prevent drying out and stress from drying out. If your plant doesn't really need water in the morning yet, but it might need water later in the day, you DAMN well should be watering it! If you don't water it right then, you will forget later on. And guess what? Your plants got all wilty and their micro roots died! Bummer, you lazy ass, you should have watered in the morning.

Watering is Marijuana 101. Do it regularly and never let your plants even think of getting dry. This one thing is the difference between tripling your harvest or not! I've seen underwatering too many times. Don't be one of those jackasses.

Splashing your plants when you water is not a great idea when they are flowering. In fact it is a very bad idea and could potentially lead to all sorts of problems. When I say splashing, I am talking about the water splashing off of the soil. When you do this it splashes soil up onto the plant which could cause mold or mildew. If your hose has so much pressure coming out of it that it always splashes you need to either turn it down or get a diffuser like a water wand.

Water wands are great because they have great reach for you to get in between the plants and they diffuse the water so you don't get a lot of runoff as long as you keep moving the wand around in a controlled and patterned motion.

So where do you want to water? Well you obviously want to water around the stock because that is where the main root ball is located. Make sure to always water that well. After that you want to water the outlying areas where you want the roots to reach to. If you are in a bed you want to water the whole bed so the roots go everywhere. Remember the bigger the roots the bigger the plant. If you are in a pot, well, water the pot!

Maintenance watering is a great idea. It keeps the health, and growth of your plants right on track. Maintenance watering is when you lightly water to maintain the optimal amount of water in your soil. This should be done at least a couple of days a week, if not every day. Obviously you don't want to do maintenance watering everyday when they are little. When the plants get bigger and want more water is when you will want to do some maintenance watering every day.

Now **deep watering** should happen at least once a week. Deep watering is when you water your plants and make sure that every cubic inch of your soil is saturated with water. Make sure to take the time to do this thoroughly and you will end up with great results. Deep watering should be done in the morning and when the soil is lightly moist and not saturated. We don't want to start over watering! When you do a deep watering it allows your plants to spread their root wings to every corner that they can reach. Which means bigger faster growth for you. This also is done to prevent the soil from drying out too much.

When you start deep watering your plants just watch how fast they grow. It is incredible to watch.

How can you possibly water every day? Think of all the time that it would take up. Relax, that is what they invented water timers and drip systems for. First, let me say if you can afford a drip system get one. They will save you hours and hours of time from having to water by hand every day.

The time you save using a timed water system will be put to good use. Namely spending that time getting and giving your plants what they need. You also will be able to spend that time searching out and destroying potential problems. If you spend your whole day just doing maintenance and work I guarantee you that you will have more problems than you know what to with. You need to automate as much as you can so you can be on the lookout for problems so you can nip them in the bud.

Even though you have an automatic watering system you still need to deep water at least once a week by hand. This keeps you in touch with the plants and allows you to check out each one on an individual basis. Another thing to mention, you need to check on your drip system at least once a week to make sure it is functioning properly and nothing is clogged. Takes about 15 to 20 minutes and, yes, you need to check it while it is on!

Checking the moisture content of your soil is a must. It should be a regular part of your routine. Checking is pretty quick and easy. If you are planted in a bed you need to check visually and physically. Just because the upper layer is wet does not mean it is wet down below. Maybe when you watered you didn't water deep enough and only the top layer was watered. I have seen this happen. Don't let this happen to you. All you need to do is dig down a bit to check for the moisture content. You will want to do this in several places to get a feel for the whole bed or beds. After checking this way for a while you will begin to develop a sense of what is occurring with your water and your soil. When you get this kind of familiarity you will be able to locate a spot or two that is fairly representative of the entire bed. What this means is if that specific spot needs water then the whole bed could use water. If you planted in pots just give them a quick lift if you can or you can use a moisture meter.

Moisture meters are an old school technology that work great, are super fast and very reliable. The meters have about a 10 inch probe you use to stick in the soil. They are affordable and they help you learn quickly how to check for moisture without disturbing your plant's roots. Once you use one for a whole season while paying attention to the plants and soil conditions you probably won't need it anymore. But your helper will!

No matter what you do there will always be a spot that gets drier faster than everywhere else. All you can really do about that spot is to pay attention and make sure it stays watered. You could add some moisture retaining material like polymer water crystals. The crystals tend to be expensive but they work great. They absorb 20 times their weight in water and release it slowly back into the soil. Have you ever seen those silly little toys you place in water and they blow up into huge gelatinous creatures? Same stuff. The crystals absorb moisture really fast so a soon as you put them into the soil and water the crystals will soak up and retain the water. Problem solved.

You will want to know the **pH balance of your water**. This way you will know if you have to treat the water in order for it to be in the appropriate pH range for your plants. pH balance stands for potential hydrogen. In this case it measures acid or base content of the water. Your target range for the pH balance of the water is 5.5 to 6.2, which is on the slightly acidic side. But hey, that's what weed likes.

There are two main ways to check the pH of your water: with a meter or with some chemicals. The meters are fast and easy. However, you have to calibrate the meters regularly in order for them to give you accurate readings. The chemical kits never need to be calibrated. Just keep them out of the direct sunlight and they will give you accurate readings every time. I recommend using the chemical kit because it's cheap, easy to use and is always accurate. The whole kit consists of a dropper with a chemical in it and a plastic vial you put water in. Fill the vial up halfway with water put in three drops of the activator and shake. Then you compare the color of the water to a little chart and you are done. You will probably check your water pH a few times a year so it's not really worth spending a $100 on a digital meter.

13 MICROBES

Beneficial microbes are the workhorses of growing plants. Beneficial microbes live in the soil and on the plant's leaves. They are microscopic organisms such as bacteria, viruses or bacilli. There a good ones (beneficial) and bad ones. They vary from location to location. What may be naturally occurring in Texas will probably be different in Oregon. This is because the microbe has evolved to live in its native environment and not someplace else.

Beneficial microbes do several different things for your plants. They help convert organic material into food for your plants. They can fight off bad microbes. Stimulate growth. Protect against lack of water by harboring water in their bodies. The list is far longer than you want to know and longer than I care to know as well. Beneficial microbes do good things for your plant. That is all you really need about them to know to grow good weed.

Do you need them to be successful? No you don't- but they do help. Especially if you are growing with organic fertilizers. If you are using chemical fertilizers the food is already available to the plants as is. Not so with organic fertilizers.

There is a saying in the industry: 'If you are using organic fertilizer you are NOT feeding the plant. You are feeding the microbes.' The microbes, in turn, are feeding the plants. This means if you are using organics you will definitely want to use beneficial microbes because they will help break down the fertilizer faster and make it available to the plant. The plant is actually eating the microbe's waste products. Talk about symbiosis.

If you don't use beneficial microbes while using organics you may inadvertently starve the plants in the worst case scenario. Best case scenario everything is fine because you had plenty of microbes in your soil already.

Do you want to take that chance? I wouldn't.

There are two categories of microbes that we will be discussing: aerobic bacteria and anaerobic bacteria.

Aerobic Bacteria

Aerobic bacteria are bacteria that require oxygen to live, grow, and divide. Aerobic bacteria fall into the "good bacteria" category because they generally do not harm the plants and in many cases do a boat load of good. Aerobic bacteria are the ones that you find in compost. They help to break down the plant material into compost.

All that the bacteria requires to create compost is food/plant waste, water, and oxygen.

The more oxygen it receives (to a point) the faster it will break down the waste material into compost. In fact the microbes are so biologically active that they can and do generate a lot of heat. If you stick your hand down into an active compost pile you could burn yourself. So be careful! Besides, it would be gross!

One of the main reasons you want to use aerobic bacteria besides breaking down food for fertilizer is they are a great defense for your soil. The idea is if you have billions of aerobic bacteria on your side then "bad" bacteria will not have a chance to compete and get established. This is a preventative measure that not only works but is well worth doing.

Anaerobic Bacteria

Anaerobic bacteria do not need oxygen to live, grow and divide. Anaerobic bacteria fall into the "bad bacteria" category because they have a tendency to harm the plant and the plants roots when they are in higher concentrations. They can help cause Fusarium wilt or root rot as well as several other diseases.

The real problem with anaerobic bacteria is how deep they live in the soil. They live deep enough that they are not getting oxygen. This means that the aerobic "good guys" die when they go into this environment. So you are stuck with potential "death zones" unless you do something about it.

If this is the case purchase an anaerobic bacteria and put that into your soil. When you do this, the anaerobic bacteria you purchased will be able to out compete the "bad guys." I recommend a product called EM1. It is fantastic and easy to use. Look it up.

The great thing about growing with the light dep technique is how fast the turnaround is from transplanting to harvest. You have a great chance of avoiding many of these problems just by the nature of your growing techniques. We are talking about a $20 investment that could save you pounds of premium smoke. You decide.

Making Compost Tea

With all this talk about beneficial microbes I bet you are wondering where to get them. This is the great part- you breed them yourself! It's pretty easy too.

What do you need to breed your own good bacteria? This obviously depends on the size of your operation. So for the sake of argument I am going to pretend that you have a light dep that is approximately 10'x20'.

You will need to produce a good amount of beneficials to water in. As a result you will need a clean and washed out 35 gallon trashcan, 30 gallons of non-chlorinated clean water, air pump, 9 pounds of compost, 6 ounces of unsulphured molasses.

You are going to make a 30 gallon batch of what is called compost tea. To make compost tea put your compost into the trashcan, add water, add a bubbler to aerate the brew, and then add unsulphured molasses. Then you let them brew for 24 hours and voila you have compost tea that you can use to inoculate your soil.

Now the trick here is to breed as many good bacteria as possible in the shortest amount of time. Here are a couple of tricks to get a head start. First you will want to prime your compost. To prime your compost you put 9 pounds of compost in a bucket and toss in the 1 cup of oatmeal too. Next you mix 1cup of water with 1 ounce of molasses. Mix thoroughly and then sprinkle it into the compost bucket and mix the compost thoroughly. Let this stand for 24 hours before using.

This will give the bacteria a head start on growing because you gave them a little bit of food and plenty of oxygen. In essence you have "primed" them for exponential growth. Exponential growth is the process of the population doubling over a given period of time. You want to start ahead of time because the first few doublings of the population don't add up to much, but once they get going watch out! Once the primed batch has sat for 24 hours in a warm location it is time to start the brewing process.

The last trick is to use water that has been heated to 70 to 80 degrees Fahrenheit. This warm temperature speeds the growth dramatically. For optimal growth you want to stay in this range. Any warmer and it's too hot and could kill the bacteria. Any colder and it's too cold for the bacteria to grow rapidly.

If you live in a city and are using city water then your water is probably chlorinated. Chlorinated water is bad for microbes. In fact the chlorine in your city water is put there to KILL microbes. That way nothing nasty starts to grow in your water. This is not a problem at all. All you need to do is fill the trashcan a day or two before brewing and the chlorine will volatize (evaporate) out of the water on its own.

To use the compost tea you just water it in to the soil. You can use it directly without diluting it or you can dilute it to a 20 to 1 ratio. 1 gallon compost tea, 20 gallons water. I would recommend no more than a 10 to 1 ratio. We really want to get a lot of beneficials in your soil to do their job. So don't dilute them too much.

REMEMBER if you are on city water to treat your water before using compost tea. Once you have finished brewing the tea it is good for about 24 hours before it goes bad. So use it quick.

Just be sure that when you use compost tea that you make certain that it soaks every inch of the soil. That way you know that the beneficials are everywhere that they need to be. I would also recommend watering your soil with regular water before you water in the compost tea. This will help reduce the surface tension of the soil. That way your compost tea will sink in instead of running off.

Recipe for Compost Tea:
Yield: 30 gallons, use within 24 hours
Materials:
   Clean 35 gallon trash can
   Air pump
Ingredients:
   30 gallons of non-chlorinated water
   9 pounds of compost
   6 ounces of unsulphured molasses
Directions:
Put compost into trash can. Add water. Use a bubbler to aerate the brew. Then add molasses. Let brew for 24 hours.

Now that you have inoculated your soil with beneficials, what's next? Remember I said that if you are using organic fertilizer that the fertilizer feeds the beneficials and their waste products will feed the plant? Well now all you have to do is add a little fertilizer to the soil. I would recommend some Azomite because it has tons of micronutrients and it is very affordable. Just top dress with it and work it in. Now you are good to go for awhile.

How often should you apply compost tea to the soil? I would say once per run, just before you plant or transplant. Spread a bunch of Azomite around and till it in. Then make a big batch of compost tea and water it in. You will want to really make sure you use a lot of the compost tea to ensure that your plants are protected. So you may have to make a couple of batches in the beginning.

If you inoculate with compost tea once per run then at most you'll do it three times a year. This is an easy solution and worth the investment of a few hours of work. Plus if you are using organic fertilizers you will have an increase in production by your plants because they aren't wasting their time trying to find food. Instead they will be using their time eating the available food and growing big ass bud!

There is an easy way to maintain the "herd" of beneficials that you have grown in your soil. In fact if you feel that your compost brewing was insufficient then you will definitely want to use this technique. All you need to do to maintain and expand your beneficial herd is occasionally water in some molasses. The molasses is another food source for your herd and when they get a hold of it they will explode in new growth.

This does not mean that you should use it every time you water. I would recommend adding molasses to your watering routine once every 2 to 3 weeks at a ratio of 1 ounce of molasses to 2 gallons of water. If you water in molasses more often than this, you will be creating an environment that could possibly be dangerous for your plants. You may be inviting in "foreign" bacteria because of all the excess molasses that is not being used.

Worse than that you could be inviting in our four footed furry friends. BEARS! Bears love sugar. And molasses is a sugar that bears can smell a mile away. Can you imagine the damage a bear could do to your garden just rooting around to find the source of that delicious smell? I don't even want to think about it and neither should you.

Not to mention that over using molasses is wasteful and adding work to your already large workload. Keep that in mind when you are applying molasses at the appropriate times, it saves you money, time and future headaches. Appropriate applications will give the herd a chance to expand and maintain a strong population which will out compete any other microbes during your run.

There is a lot of hype when it comes to compost tea and beneficial bacteria. If you listen and read articles you (along with the world) will be lead to believe that compost tea is the panacea for all that ails your plant. In fact, if you don't use compost tea you are killing the world and all that's in it. Okay, I may be dramatizing the situation a bit. But only a bit.

Compost tea won't cure everything that ails you plant, but it does help.

I know people who brew a batch and water with it once a week. Their philosophy is: if a little is good then more is great! With compost tea, if you are brewing it correctly, there is absolutely no danger to your plants. Your soil gets inoculated and the plants do get a small amount of fertilizer. BUT EVERY WEEK!? "Come on!" is what I say. Don't you have better things to do with your time (like spend it with the ones you love)? You seriously could use compost tea once a week. But there are more effective uses for your time and energy.

Have you ever heard of carrying capacity? This is the idea that any given environment can only support so much life and no more than that. My point is every time those people brew their weekly batch of compost tea and water it into the soil, when have they reached carrying capacity? It is a scientific fact that they WILL reach it quickly if they keep applying it weekly.

Once carrying capacity is reached the overpopulation dies off. There are not enough resources for them to survive so their only choice is to die off. This isn't necessarily bad. When they die they become food for the plants. But weren't they already supplying food through their actions anyway?

Before the overpopulation dies off they will try and consume as much food as possible in order to live, which means they convert the fertilizer into usable food for your plants. The problem with that is your plants already had enough food before the overpopulation explosion. So now you have fertilizer that is going to be wasted. Your plant can't consume more just because there is more available. My point is once you have reached carrying capacity anything that you add after that is just a waste of time, money and effort. Don't fall for the hype of more > better > best.

When you brew compost tea you are brewing up a batch of bio-diversity that is quite amazing. You will have hundreds of different aerobic bacteria at your beck and call. Not to mention different types of fungi that are great for your plants. Depending on how you brew your batch you can focus more on a bacterial tea or a fungus tea. The difference is in how long you brew the tea.

I did not discuss this in the recipe section because there is no reason too. Sure you will hear plenty of people who will say, "A bacterial tea will do X during this stage of the plants lifecycle and a fungus tea will do X during this stage of the lifecycle." While those statements are true, the idea that you need to brew specific batches during different stages of life is crazy. All you need is a general compost tea recipe that grows both fungus and bacteria. This is the recipe I gave you.

Why do I believe you only need a general recipe instead of a fungus or bacterial tea? Because I trust in Mother Nature to know what the fuck she is doing. These beneficials have been around for thousands of years. They know how to survive in adverse conditions, which your garden is NOT! No, your garden is paradise for these little fuckers! And you created those conditions on purpose.

What I'm trying to say is this. When you pour your compost tea on the soil a certain percent are going to be active and a certain percent will go dormant. The dormant ones are waiting for the right conditions to become active and when those occur they will become active. You should trust Mother Nature too. Just supply the population with a good environment and let Mother Nature do the rest.

Chemical fertilizers and beneficial microbes

Can they coexist or do chemical fertilizers kill the beneficials? The answer is, strangely enough, both are true. They can coexist together and chemical fertilizers will kill beneficial microbes.

The common misconception is that they cannot coexist together. The common belief is that chemical fertilizers will kill the bacteria when you use it on the soil. That using chemical fertilizers kill the soil with no chance of recovery. This is hardly the truth. When you apply chemical fertilizers in low doses you are fine. The beneficials will actually use the chemical fertilizers as a food source as well.

The key to successful coexistence is using chemical fertilizer in low doses. That's it. Now if you follow the application directions on the chemical fertilizers packages you will kill your soil and your bacteria. You will also potentially create a toxic build up in the soil following the manufacturer's directions.

Remember manufacturers are in the business of selling fertilizer and not in the business of keeping your soil alive. When the chemical fertilizer companies created their proprietary blend of fertilizers they didn't once concern themselves with the effects of the fertilizer on the bacteria in the soil. And why would they? The idea is that the chemical fertilizer provides everything the plant needs instantly, without using the microbes. So what if they kill the microbes? No big deal right?

WRONG! The microbes do more than convert organic material into usable food for plants. They recondition the soil, hold in extra moisture (in their bodies), fight off bad microbes and a whole slew of things that science has yet to discover.

So feel good about using chemical fertilizers, as long as you use them responsibly. This means at least halving the dose if not more. I personally use about an 1/8 of the recommended dose, but I feed my plants more often to compensate for the low dose.

Remember by using microbes you are effectively enlisting volunteers that are willing to give your plants ideal living conditions. So do the responsible thing and get your free labor force today.

14 VEGETATIVE GROWTH

The purpose of vegetative growth in marijuana is to produce new growth without producing flowers. During vegetative growth the plant is producing new leaves, branches, stalks and roots. The leaves are used to capture the sun's light in order to convert that light into energy for growth production. The new branches are used to increase the diameter of the plant. The new stalk is used to support the plant itself. And the new root growth is used to collect more food to support the growth of the plant.

Normally vegetative growth occurs naturally in midspring to midsummer. This is due to the hours of sunlight available to the plant. The hours of sunlight available during this period range from 14 hours to 18 hours of sunlight, depending on your location.

So what is the purpose of vegetative growth? The point is for the plant to grow as large as possible before fall. The larger the plant grows the more branches and nodal sites it creates. The more branches and nodal sites that the plant produces, the greater the chance that the plant has to create flowers. This is because the branches and nodal sites are the locations in which the plant will create flowers. The plant has evolved over thousands of years to make the most of sunlight during those months and grow, grow, grow.

The light requirement for marijuana to stay in vegetative growth depends on the variety of course! But in general, if you give your plants more than 14.5 hours of continuous light the plants will stay in vegetative growth. The plants are obviously very sensitive to light, the light intensity, and the duration of the light.

As I said there are some varieties that will actually start to flower/preflower if they are given only 14.5 hours of continuous light. So you really need to be careful when choosing a strain. Find out as much as you can about the strain you are interested in to avoid this problem.

If you have plants under 18 or more hours of continuous light and you want to put them under 14.5 hours of continuous light you must harden them off. If you do not harden your plants off they will more than likely start to flower.

So what is hardening off? **Hardening off** is the process of slowly matching up the light cycles. For example if your plants are at 24 hours of light you will want to use a 3 to 4 week process to sync up the light cycles. Week 1 you would drop your lights to 18 hours a day. Week 2 you drop the time by 1.5 hours. So you would be at 16.5 hours. Week 3 you would drop an hour and be at 15.5 hours of continuous light. And week 4 you would drop another hour and end up at 14.5 hours of continuous light.

It is very important to take your time to harden your plants off if you are going to switch to just using the sun. This process will really help to boost your harvest to where you want to be.

During the vegetative state you will want to tailor your food to meet the plant's requirements. Throughout every stage of the plant's life cycle the plant will have different nutrient requirements. When the plant is in the vegetative state and given optimal conditions (light, heat, water, air) the plants will consume a lot of the element nitrogen. This is classic for vegetative growth.

Of course, the plant will also require phosphorous and potassium and all the other nutrients as well. So you will want to find a fertilizer high in nitrogen that also has a good ratio balance between the three macro fertilizers.

What exactly does that mean? Remember how we discussed the numbers on the fertilizer containers? They look something like this. 3-1-2 and they stand for N-P-K (nitrogen, phosphorous, potassium) in that order. Always. Those numbers are a ratio of the fertilizer contained within. There is said to be a perfect ratio for growing marijuana and I actually agree with that, but with a caveat. There is a perfect ratio for each strain, because each strain is different and has different nutrient requirements.

Don't despair there is a WIDE RANGE of nutrient ratios that will work just fine. A common ratio that is considered a good one for vegetative growth is 3-1-2. This means any fertilizer that falls in this ratio is good. What? Well if you multiply the 3-1-2 by 1 you get 3-1-2. If you multiply it by 2 you get 6-2-4. And if you multiply it by 6 you get 18-6-12 and so on… The numbers have increased but the ratio remains the same. Just keep in mind that there are plenty of other ratios out there that work just as well. Find what works for you in your area.

Now you are giving your plants everything they need during this stage (light, heat, water, air, food) and they look great. Right? At this stage they should be vibrant, healthy, and growing vigorously. This is for all the marbles so make sure that your plants are in a lush happy environment because you are setting the stage for your future harvests. Make sure you are firing on all cylinders.

If for some reason your plants are not firing on all cylinders you need to do some serious investigating. I'm talking serious. You need to look for the obvious signs such as yellowing of the leaves, stunted growth when compared to others plants and overwatering.

I can't say it enough; overwatering is the number one culprit for slow growth for beginners. Remember to let your plants go from wet to moist. At this stage they should be in pots so you'll want to pick up the pots. If it's heavy let it dry out a little bit before watering it again.

Why am I harping on getting your plants in to kickass mode? Because every day that your plants aren't in kickass mode it puts you behind by a week. Every bad day equals a week of being behind. This is such a shitty place to be and I don't want you to ever experience it.

The best part is, it is almost 100% avoidable. So do some investigating to find the cause of your case of slow growth. If the plants aren't getting enough light, make sure they get it. If the plants are too cold put a small greenhouse over them to keep them warm (especially in the spring).

Whatever the problem is figure it out and get back on course and I promise you that you'll be rewarded.

Roots. They are the beginning and the end of it all. My friend tells me often, "You are not growing weed you are growing roots. If your roots are happy then your whole plant is happy." At first I didn't get it but over time I did. The bigger your roots are and the healthier they are the faster your plants will grow. He probably should have said that instead. Oh well.

What do you need to know about your roots? Keep the temperature of the root zone between 65 to 72 degrees Fahrenheit. This is the range at which the plants will grow their roots and their vegetative material fastest.

If your temperature in the root zone falls below 65 degrees Fahrenheit, your growth will slow down dramatically. Now, if your plants get too warm this slows down growth as well and opens you up to all sorts of root diseases. So keep your plant roots in the safe zone of 65 to 72 degrees Fahrenheit for optimal hassle free performance.

Root bound plants are a potential problem, especially if you are giving your plants the optimal conditions. Root bound occurs when the plants roots fill the container so full that there is no place for them to grow more. In essence they maxed out their space.

Sounds like a good thing doesn't it? Your plants grew so much they filled the container! There is a downside to this. When your plants are root bound they slow their growth and settle into what I call survival mode. The plant knows that it has achieved max capacity and at this point is just trying to survive instead of putting on new growth. Root bound plants require additional watering because there isn't enough dirt to hold water.

Transplanting is the answer. All you need to do is transplant into a bigger pot or bed to get your plants back on track. Well, there is one more thing you'll need to do to trigger your plants vigorous growth. You will need to DAMAGE THE ROOTBALL. You heard me right you will have to damage the root ball in order to encourage new growth. Typically when a plant is root bound the roots start a circular pattern around the root ball. If this is the case you will be able to see it clear as day. All you need to do it peel off about a ¼ to ½ inch off of the root ball all the way around the circumference. Now just replant it and water. Your plant will recover from the shock in a couple of days and the roots will start growing out instead of continuing the circular pattern. This will initiate new growth up above as well.

During the spring you want to ensure that plants are growing nice and fast. However, early spring has many inborn enemies to the light dep grower. Namely short days and long nights. We already discussed the problems of short day and how to cure them. What about long nights? The major problem with long nights, besides the dark, are cold nights. I don't know if you have paid attention to the morning temperatures in early spring but they are cold. Far colder than your plants can handle without protection. You need to make sure that your plants don't get too cold at night. The optimal temperature range is 60 to 85 degrees Fahrenheit.

I know that that temperature range is pretty much impossible to achieve during early spring. Don't freak out about it too much. Just do the best you can. I've seen plants go down into the 50's at night and they still performed well. But steps were to make sure they didn't go any lower than that.

A small greenhouse was made with PVC pipe and then covered with clear platic. When the temperatures kept dropping another greenhouse was put over that one. That did the trick! During the day when it was maybe 50 degrees Fahrenheit, it was a toasty 80 degrees in the double layered greenhouse. Let me tell you those plants exploded with growth when the temperature was raised up a notch or two. During the night the plants dropped into the 50's but it was for just a couple of hours a day before the sun came out and heated everything up again.

During those long nights in spring it is important to do some light breaking to achieve the growth you need in order to get the yield you want. I have always recommended light breaks at 1 in the morning for an hour or two especially in crowded neighborhood areas. Less people are out and about at 1 in the morning. If someone is up they usually just figured you left your light on accidentally. However, you could do light breaking in the morning and evening in order to mimic the spring time planting conditions. It is entirely up to you. There is no wrong answer here as long as you do it.

The goal is to keep the plants growing without interruption. Every time your beautiful babies experience an interruption of growth it really sets you back for weeks. Accidents happen and nothing runs exactly as it should, so you need to account for that by getting started earlier and growing more plants than you think you need. Grow 10-20% more plants than you need because shit happens. I am always pleased with the results by hedging my bets.

Speaking of hedging your bets, you should pinch the tops of your plants to encourage your plant to grow wider instead of taller. By pinching the tops of your plants during vegetative growth you will encourage lateral growth which will create more top buds. More tops is a lot better than one big ass bud up top. Yes, a big ass bud looks impressive, but more tops means more smoke for you. So go ahead and grow one big ass plant and top the rest. Besides, the taller your plants are the more likely they are to get damaged by the plastic as it is pulled over the frame. And they are more manageable when they are smaller.

To encourage growth and health you should spray your plants with a foliar spray once a week. The foliar spray should be a supplemental food source for the plant. Did you know that your plants absorb nutrients through their leaves? In essence your plant up top is a secondary root system that can help feed the plant.

If you ever experience a nutrient deficiency the fastest way to help your plant is to spray them with some fertilizer. The plant will absorb the nutrients and use it appropriately. Of course you will want to fertilize your plant through the soil as well.

Another benefit of spraying your plants is pest control. Just coating pests in water regularly is a great way to help control the pests before they get out of control. So include a regular maintenance spraying in your routine during the vegetative state of the plants for optimal growth.

Remember a happy healthy plant creates its own defense against pests and problems. Achieving a bunch of happy healthy plants is well within your skill set. Yes, it will take work and time. If you give your plants the time and energy they require they will in return give you some amazing bud in return.

16 FLOWERING

The purpose of flowering in marijuana is to secure the next generation of offspring (seeds). Well, for our purpose it is to create some primo bud and not to produce seed. Because we are not trying to breed seed flowering is the final stage of the plant's lifecycle as far as we are concerned. After the plant is finished flowering we will harvest, cure and manicure the plant. But all those steps take place after the plant is dead.

The basic characteristics of a flowering marijuana plant are the shortening of nodal spacing, slowing and then stopping of vegetative growth and producing flowers. The plant has a lot to do in 8 to 10 short weeks, so we need to make sure that they get everything they need.

The nodal spacing of a flowering plant becomes shorter because the plant is or has transitioned out of vegetative state and is in the flowering state. What happens is the plants energy is now solely focused on creating new flowers instead of new growth. So the shortening of the nodal spacing is really just a side effect of the plants genetic imperative to flower.

Triggering marijuana into flowering is no secret and we have already discussed it in this book. But for those of you who like to skip around in books here is the secret. To trigger the plants to flower you must give the plants 12 or more hours of UNITERRUPTED darkness on a daily basis. When they receive their night schedule it should start at the same time everyday and end at the same time every day. This is better for the plant and makes it is easier on you when you have a set routine that allows you to memorize your schedule. A schedule will help reduce mistakes and human error.

Now, some strains are more light sensitive than other strains. Just make sure to do your due diligence on what strains you are going to be using. Find out their light requirements and there should be no problems.

However, a schedule of 12 hours of uninterrupted darkness is a catchall schedule. This means 12 hours of darkness will pretty much trigger every marijuana plant to flower. So if you don't want to just use the 12 hours of darkness make sure that you know exactly how much your strain requires. This is not something you want to guess at.

Fertilizing during flowering

During flower your plants will require a completely different fertilizer ratio. The plants are now focusing their energy on creating flowers versus new growth. In order to create flowers, the plant needs a fertilizer that is heavy in phosphorous. A good N-P-K ratio is 1-3-2. Any variation of this ratio would be just fine (e.g. 2-6-4, 3-9-6, 4-12-8). Like I said before: this is just a suggestion. There are many formula ratios out there that will work for you. Find what you like and stick with it to achieve the best results.

Many people are firm believers that you should quit giving your plants nitrogen during the flowering stage. I am not one of those. Experiments over the years and have found that not giving the plants nitrogen during flowering reduces your overall yield. Let me repeat that in simpler terms: NO NITROGEN = SMALLER YIELD. If you are cool with that, more power to you. Not me.

I'm sure plenty of people will say something like "But the quality of the smoke is superior when you stop using nitrogen during flower." That may or may not be the case. But I know for a fact you would rather have two times as much A quality bud than half as much A+ quality bud. The quality difference is half a grade at best.

Back to the food demands of the plant. I'll give you a quick and easy guide to follow when fertilizing during flowering:

Week 1: continue to use vegetative fertilizer
Week 2 and 3: use half vegetative fertilizer and half bloom fertilizer
Week 4-9: use bloom fertilizer

That is a pretty simple schedule that I have seen work. The reason you want to continue to use grow fertilizer is to encourage your plants to grow to fill the space.

Everything you do just before flowering is crucial to what your end results will be. Always remember that. When you transplant your plants into their final location you want to make sure that you choose the healthiest plants to put in your light dep.

Transplanting

Your transplanting schedule is going to be very crucial. The timing is very important. You want to make sure that the plants are on the fast track. Growing kick ass style. If they aren't there yet make sure to get them there before you transplant them. This is why I suggested that you grow 10-20% extra plants. Because some will get stunted and some will die. It just happens. MOVE ON.

One of the worst things you can do is transplant too late. Why? Because you have to worry about your plants being root bound. Yes, they'll recover if you use the proper technique discussed earlier, but it will set you back about 1-2 weeks. If you plant too early you just have to wait for your plants to grow into the space. How long will that take? That depends on how small your plants were to begin with. But if it's the first run, and you have the proper set up to keep them happy, I say go ahead and plant a little early and let them get established.

Well now they are all nice and cozy in their final location. You want to make sure that you baby these girls along for at least a week. They just went through some trauma when you transplanted them. Yes, transplanting is a form of trauma. Maybe you did it right and the trauma was minimal, and maybe it was very traumatic.

I have seen and done things in the transplanting world that I am not proud of. It is very easy to transplant as long as you have a good technique. It took me time to develop a good technique. There was a lot of trial and error that went into this one but I feel I finally nailed it down a few years ago.

Here is a good transplanting method:

Step 1: Check the moisture content of the plant. If it has just been watered wait until the root ball is drier because soaking wet root balls tend to fall apart!

Step 2: Dig a hole.

Step 3: While plant is still in the original pot place the plant into the hole you dug. Does it fit? Yes? Good! If not dig some more until it fits.

Step 4: Remove plant from pot by placing the stem of the plant between the base of your pointer and middle fingers. Now turn the pot upside down and gently tap the edge of the pot upwards on ALL sides. This should make the pot come off easily.

Step 5: Using TWO HANDS gently place plant in hole. DO NOT SLAM IT IN!! (I have actually watched people do this. Groan.)

Step 6: Gently back fill the hold with soil.

Step 7: Water your plants until saturated.

What do you think? Only took me a few years to get my head out of my ass! Just follow this technique and you will have great results.

Some other transplanting tips: Pre-water the soil you are planting in the day before. Transplant in the late afternoon closer to sunset. This gives your plants some transition time before they have to start converting sunlight to energy.

So you've transplanted and got your plants acclimated to their new environment, now it's time to turn the lights down and get the party started! This is generally considered the most exciting time of all. Flowering! But before flowering is pre-flowering. This is the period of time when the plants are transitioning from vegetative growth to flowering. This period will last anywhere from 1 to 3 weeks depending on the strain. Generally speaking a strain that flowers in 8 weeks will preflower 1 to 2 weeks and a 10 week strain will preflower for 3 weeks.

Understanding your plants pre-flowering characteristics is really important. You want to know how much they are going to stretch before they go into full flower. If you know how much they are going to stretch you will be able to determine exactly how big to grow them before you turn them down to flower. You don't want to waste your time growing them too big or too small. If you grow them too big you are just wasting time and nutrients. Not to mention the additional maintenance labor you created for yourself. If you flipped (turned down the lights to induce flowering) when they were too small then you end up with a smaller yield, which sucks when you consider all the hard work that you already put in. So learn your preflower growth!

Maintenance spraying of your plants during preflower is okay. You will not hurt them at all as long as you spray at the appropriate time of day. In fact, you can spray your plants safely up to 4 weeks into flower. Anything after that I would not recommend, it is far too dangerous to your plant's health.

The best time to spray your plants when they are in flower is the early morning before any direct sunlight hits them. This gives the moisture that you have sprayed on them the chance to evaporate slowly. The process is similar to the morning dew evaporating off the plants in the morning. The idea is to mimic what naturally happens in nature. If it works for nature it will work for you.

The danger of spraying later in the day when direct sunlight is on the flower is the chance of burning your flowers. When you burn your flowers the two white hairs shrivel up and turn brown. This is a big problem because now your plants think they have been impregnated. This is called a false pregnancy and during a false pregnancy your plants will shift their energy from making new flowers to creating a seed that doesn't exist. So instead of big ass bud you end up with some very nice small bud! Don't let this happen to you.

Maintenance at this stage is key, because if you falter in any major way you will lose massive weight in bud. So keep on your shit. You are in the last legs and everything needs to be taken care of pronto. Follow your schedule and pay attention to detail. It is simple enough and the rewards are spectacular!

Make sure to water regularly and don't let them wilt. If you let them dry out too much the hairs on your flowers will die and BAM false pregnancy! You know that story already.

Don't let it get too hot when you are covering your plants. Why? The hairs will die and BAM false pregnancy. If you need to vent while covered then you should do that. You want to avoid temperatures over 100 degrees Fahrenheit for extended periods of time.

Make sure everything is running just so. You want to keep everything in the happy middle. Nothing too extreme on either side of the pendulum. Not too hot or too cold. Not too wet or too dry. Not overfed or underfed. You want it just right.

I know it takes time to learn exactly where that is, but as long as you pay attention you'll find it rather quickly.

If you don't stick to the middle of the road you are introducing high levels of stress to your garden. This is bad and should be avoided at all costs. The major sources of stress are soaring temperatures, under watering and interrupting the light cycle.

Hermaphrodites

When your plant goes into stress mode it goes into fight or flight mode. Since it can't fly away it has no choice but to go into fight mode. What does this entail? The plant's mode of fighting is to shut down growth. All growth. At this point it is going to do anything in its power to protect everything that it has already created (e.g. flowers) in the hopes of producing viable offspring.

So what does that mean in the real world? It means the plant will focus on producing seed by producing the dreaded hermaphrodite. Your beautiful female will start to grow male flowers in order to reproduce viable off spring.

When this happens you have a couple of choices. Cut out the male part or kill the whole plant. I prefer to kill the whole plant because there is less to worry about in the long run. If you don't destroy the whole plant you will have to check that plant every couple of days just to make sure that it has not started producing new male flowers. If you don't constantly monitor that plant it may spread some pollen over the entire light dep garden.

Can you imagine how fucked up that would be? Weeks away from harvest and your crop is toast.

Do yourself a favor and don't stress your plants. If you do and a hermaphrodite appears kill the damn thing!

Stressing your plants is not the only way that the hermaphrodites pop up. Some strains are genetically predisposed to producing hermaphrodites. Only some. You just need to pay attention to what you are growing and checking your crop once a week for male flowers.

Plants that will occasionally produce 1 or 2 male flowers at a nodal intersection. Just pinch off the male flowers and move on. But I'm literally talking about 1 or 2 flowers, not an entire branch. If it is an entire branch just kill the whole damn plant. It ain't worth it to play around! Protect what you've got, not what you little extra you'll get.

So now you've got a stress free environment! That's great. Just make sure to keep your roots happy too. You already know how to do it with everything we have already covered.

I just want to add this little tidbit about roots and flowering:

If you are flowering in pots and your plants become root bound, it is okay. You are so close to the end that it won't matter except you will probably have to water a bit more. Just continue to monitor your plants like you always have.

There is a side effect of your plants being root bound when they flower and it is a good side effect. The plants that are root bound tend to flower harder and faster. They produce big ass buds that finish a week or so sooner than plants that aren't root bound! It's crazy the things you learn over time just by being observant.

In fact, if your plants get too root bound before flowering the root boundness actually shifts the plant into pre-flowering. Another good reason to transplant your vegetative plants on schedule.

Cutting in Light

If you have timed everything just right, you will need to cut in some light. The reason you want to cut in light is to produce bigger better buds. The best time to cut in light is right after pre-flowering has finished. This is the best time because the plant has stopped stretching and growing and is now solely focused on producing flowers.

So what do I mean when I say cut in light? I mean to literally cut out branches that are not going to produce anything because they are shaded out by upper branches. Sometimes you even need to cut out some upper branches to achieve the best yield. This is a skill that takes awhile to learn because it is counter intuitive.

Whenever I teach someone about cutting in light that has never done it I get a good laugh out of it. Without fail, I mean without fail, a newbie will freak out when watching me cut out branches. Especially when it's branch, after branch, after branch on the same plant. They think that I have lost my mind. The best is when I get invited over to their garden and I give them the business. They fricken loose their minds! So I only do one or two plants and then I say, "Alright lets mark these two and compare the yields to the other stuff after harvest".

It's weird that after that lesson they start using my technique from then on. Must be because it works! To be honest the first time I did it I freaked out too. But now I know why it works.

It works because your plant has only so much energy and food to produce bud. Now that energy will be split up into however many bud sites that there are. Obviously, the buds in the sunlight are going to get more energy from the plant than the buds in the shade. This means the buds in the shade ARE going to redirect a certain portion of that food and energy into their little budlets. Well those budlets are crap! They are too small to amount to anything so all they really do is suck up energy and produce nothing.

Your job is to cut out those branches below that are not going to receive direct sunlight. Now don't go hog wild and cut out everything. Just get in there and cut out the branches that aren't going to produce anything. If you have a long branch with the end that is exposed to light, but the rest isn't, clean up the interior part and leave the top.

The idea is to focus the plant's energy into the buds in the light so that they get bigger and better. For light dep I have noticed that the best depth of a canopy is approximately 2 feet to 2.5 feet. If your canopy is thicker than 2 feet to 2.5 feet you are just wasting the plants energy.

The thickness of the canopy depends on the type of strain. If, for example, you have a Sour Diesel you can let your canopy get even a little thicker because the plant's nature is to stretch out so that light will penetrate deeply. If, on the other hand, you are running a Bubba Kush your canopy depth is probably gonna be around two feet. Heavy indica varieties, such as Bubba Kush, have big ass leaves. I'm talking big!

Anyways, you will need to deleaf the big water leaves in order for the light to penetrate through the canopy. Those leaves are so big they literally shade out anything below it so you need to go through and pinch off as many water leaves as possible.

You will want to wait until after preflower to pinch the leaves because that is when the plant stops stretching. When you do deleaf, I want you to do it hard! I mean hard. Take off every big water leaf and go back in two weeks. Your plant won't even look like it was ever deleafed.

I recommend deleafing once or twice during flowering. You will want to wait until after preflower or you will just have to do it again to get the light penetration you need.

Right after you cut in some light, or debranching your garden, you will want to support your plants. There are numerous ways to do it. The best way to do it is the way that allows you the most access while being the easiest to put into place.

Most people will get trellis netting and place it horizontally over the canopy. The netting is supported on the sides with the hoops that are already in place. Just use a few zip ties here and there. You will also want to do it in manageable sections. Try to force the tops of the plants through the netting at least 6 to 12 inches.

This will offer great stability and prevent the plant and branches from breaking because your buds got too heavy. Or if it rains. A good rain will snap unsupported plants in a heartbeat. Use whatever technique works for you. Just make sure to support your plants before they snap!

16 VENTILATION

Just like humans, plants need to breathe in order to survive. Plants breathe in carbon dioxide and exhale oxygen. The carbon dioxide that your plants breathe comes from the air in the atmosphere. Only a tiny percentage of the atmosphere is made up of carbon dioxide. The atmosphere is made up primarily of nitrogen (78%) and oxygen (21%). The rest of the 1% of the atmosphere is made up of everything else combined. Where does carbon dioxide fall in that 1% soup? The percentage of carbon dioxide in the atmosphere is 0.039%. As you can see it is a rather small number and yet the entire plant population of the world depends on it.

Fresh air is a must in order for your plants to thrive. Fresh air carries more than just air. Air carries moisture, pathogens and other teeny tiny solids. There really isn't much you can do about the things that are in the air. It would be really hard to treat you air on a large scale. It can be done, it would just be very energy intensive and costly. There really is no need to do that if you are growing in the right times of the year. Namely late spring through early fall. If you are growing during this time, the air is already in pretty good condition because of Mother Nature. If you choose to grow in the other parts of the seasons it would behoove you to condition your air. You will want to remove moisture because the air during late fall to spring is full of mold spores due to the increased moisture in the air.

Now, getting fresh air during the day when you are light depping is no problem. Your plants are constantly exposed to the outside air. However, when your plants are covered it is a different story. I am assuming that your plants are being covered by a non permeable light proof plastic. Let me say that this is okay. But during the hours that your greenhouse is covered your plants are still transpiring water not to mention the moisture being evaporated from the ground.

Imagine, if you will, the plastic is pulled and it is pitch black, the air is FULL of moisture (I mean FULL), and the temperature is rising. Suddenly we went from 80 degrees to 95 degrees in a matter of minutes. Can you picture it? Can you feel it? Good.

Guess who loves those exact conditions? Mold! That's who. So we have created a perfect storm to breed mold on a daily basis. This is not good and needs to be addressed. The best way to solve this problem is to ventilate the light dep. Venting will reduce the moisture build up and reduce the internal temperature.

If you do not vent you are risking damage to your plants by exposing them to powdery mildew, mold and heat. Let me tell you right now heat is no joke. Heat will stunt your plants like no other. The real tricky part about the heat problem is it is hard to detect. The signs are subtle. It doesn't look like anything is wrong except your plants aren't growing. Hopefully you catch the problem before it starts to stunt your plants. Do not let your plants get over 100 degrees Fahrenheit unless it is 100 degrees outside. Then it is unavoidable. I've seen heat damage a few times. The expected yield was cut in half! Could you live with less than half your expected yield? Especially knowing it is curable? It makes for a miserable year let me tell you.

If you vent during the covered hours you can solve this problem. When you vent you will want to make sure the outtake is at the highest point it can be at. Also make sure it is on one of the ends and not in the middle. This is because it is easier to place an outtake on the ends rather than the middle. You will want to place your intake on the opposite end so that you get airflow all the way through the light dep.

The point of venting for the light dep is not to give the plants fresh air. The point is to remove moisture and to remove heat. It is important to remember that, because if there wasn't a heat or moisture buildup you wouldn't be venting at all. It's not like your plants have a high air demand when there is no light source. Also, your plants are only going to be covered for a few hours so really nothing to worry about as far as carbon dioxide is concerned.

When you are venting don't expect the temperatures to drop to be the same as outside air temperatures. That is unrealistic, but you can expect a significant temperature drop that will stabilize with venting. That is all you need to protect your crops.

To vent you will need to use fans to pull out the hot, humid air. If you are off grid you are going to need to get solar powered fans unless you have a generator. If you are on grid you just need to get some AC vent fans. The real trick is light proofing the intakes and outtakes. You have to decide how you want to do it. Have ducting going under the plastic… build solid end walls and attach light baffles. There are several ways to do it and you need to decide what way is right for you.

You can expect the humidity to behave in a similar fashion when venting. The humidity will drop while venting, and stabilize to a degree, but don't expect the inside humidity to be the same as the outside humidity. This is because of all the evaporation and transpiration occurring inside the covered structure.

Your target humidity range is between 40% and 50%. Within this range your plants will be happy whether they are budding or not, because they will still be absorbing water from the roots. When the humidity is too low, around 10%, the plant will close its pores or stomata to protect itself from dehydration. This will result in your plants stagnating because they are unable to drink more water to grow. On the other hand, if you expose your plants to too much moisture you have a GREAT opportunity to give your plants a case of powdery mildew or mold.

Just to be clear you probably will not be able to keep your plants within the humidity target range (40-50%) the whole time. There will be periods where they are living outside of the range. This is okay as long as it is not for twelve hours or more in a row. Obviously you want to minimize the time the plants are outside of the target humidity range.

Since exposing your plants to high temperatures is sometimes unavoidable it is important to understand what heat can do to your plants. During the heat of the summer sometimes the temperature soars and you may expose your plants to 100+ degrees. When this happens your plant shuts down. The plant closes its pores to stop transpiration. This effectively stops growth during this high temp period. Now imagine this heat wave lasting two weeks. This means your plants loose two weeks of growth! That is gonna reduce your yield for sure! If for some reason your plant's pores don't close down then you could have the opposite problem. To deal with the heat your plant will start sucking up as much water as it can to cool itself off. So your plant may dry out because it sucked up all the water and you didn't plan on watering again for a couple of days!

In the heat of the summer you need to be paying attention! But what is worse than the last scenario is this: Imagine you just fertilized and a heat wave strikes. Your plants start sucking up water by the boatloads and along with the water. The plant is sucking up all that fertilizer and BAM! You just fertilizer burned your plants. Doesn't matter that you gave your plants the recommended dose that isn't supposed to burn them. It did- and they are toast!

Just another good reason to cut your fertilizer strength in half or more!

On the flip side of hot weather is cold weather. If you are experiencing cold weather, there is absolutely no reason to vent! This is the time when you want to trap that heat in to protect the plants. In fact if the outside temperature is too cool you may want to leave the plastic on overnight.

During the spring when you first start to pull the tarp over I would definitely recommend keeping the plastic on overnight for the first month of pulling unless you are having nights that are above 60 degrees Fahrenheit. This will keep your girls nice and warm in the nights and allow them to start up earlier in the morning. During the first month you don't have to worry about mold as long as the outside temperatures are cool. This will give your plants a nice "head start".

The first month of flower you don't have to worry about mold because the flowers are not too dense at this point. You need to start worrying about mold after week four of the flowering cycle when the flowers are stacking and becoming dense.

With all this said about venting and the importance of venting, let me say this: I have seen some KILLER BUD that had no venting during the covered cycle. This was done because the person was able to minimize the heat and humidity build up by covering during the cooler times of the day. This meant more work, because they had to cover twice a day and uncover twice a day, but the results were/are amazing. If you aren't afraid of some hard work this method will work for you.

17 SOIL

Soil is the medium of choice for people who grow light dep. And that is what I recommend that you use. Of course now we need to discuss all the aspects of soil that need to be considered. The three factors that I mostly look for in soil are: density, moisture retention, and longevity.

The **density** of soil is important from a root stand point. If the soil is very dense then the roots will not be able to extend into the soil easily. If the roots can't extend into soil easily and expand then the roots will be "stunted" which means your plant will also be stunted. Remember we are working with a small window of time for the plants to do their thing. We are talking 9 to 11 weeks. That is not much time so we want to make sure the plants don't have to fight to get their roots big. The bigger the roots, the bigger the plant.

Longevity in a soil is important because you don't want to be replacing it every year. That is a lot of money and a lot of work. You are looking for soil that doesn't quickly break down and start compacting. If your soil breaks down fast and starts to compact your roots won't be able to grow quickly and easily which will lead to stunted plants. The plants won't look stunted because they will be healthy but they could have been a lot bigger if the roots had a chance to grow with ease.

The way to deal with soil that breaks down fast is to add soil conditioners before the season starts. You will want to add some compost to the soil and mix it thoroughly in. This will lighten the soil dramatically and allow your roots to once again grow with ease.

A soil that is light and fluffy will allow the roots to grow and extend with ease. However soils that are light and fluffy tend not to retain moisture. This means you will have to water more often.

What you are looking for is a soil that is not too dense, that can retain a good amount of moisture, and will last a long time (i.e. won't degrade and compact after one season). The great news is there are a lot of soils out there just like this. They are called potting soil or planting mixes.

Many potting soils and planting mixes come pre-amended. This means that the soil has fertilizer already mixed in. The manufacturers have all sorts of blends that they make and use. Blends for seedlings, blends for cuttings, blends for vegetative growth, blends for flowering... You name it and they probably have it.

I do not like pre-amended soils! I really don't. Maybe it is because I don't buy soil that often and I don't really want to learn the ins and outs of one particular brand. Or maybe it's because I buy in bulk and can only get what that company has available. Either way the end result is the same. I don't like pre-amended soils because I don't know what's in there. I don't know how long it's going to last. I don't know if it is going to burn my plants.

Basically, I just DON'T KNOW WHAT'S IN THERE!! So I prefer to get soil that doesn't have anything in it. I know how to mix my fertilizers and when to use them. I don't want to count on someone else's blends. I know mine works and when to use it. That is something I can count on. So I don't buy pre-amended soil.

You, on the other hand, can buy pre-amended soils or you can choose to take control of your plants from Day 1 and give them what they need. You know my thoughts: no pre-amended soil!

There are a lot of soils out there. What makes one better than another? Is the expensive soil better than the cheaper one?

What you need to do is judge the characteristics of the soil. Ask yourself and answer these questions about the soil: Is it too light and fluffy? Is it too dense? Are the particles too big? Are the particles too small?

If you answer these questions and judge the soils against each other based on these questions you will find the right soil for you rather quickly.

Just because a soil is expensive does not make it the best choice. It just makes it expensive. Usually expensive soil is pre-amended and that can lead to problems. One time I bought 40 cubic yards of some pre-amended soil. Planted my plants and promptly burned the hell out of them. You would think that a company wouldn't sell you soil that is so hot that it could actually burn your plants. Well they can and they do!

So be careful and don't get BURNED! (Get it?!)

Used soil is a wonderful thing. I have had great success using "used" soil. I got it from a local landscape materials supply company. They would allow people to come by and drop off their used soil for a fee. The soil came from indoor and outdoor growers. It also came from landscapers looking to get rid of soil from jobs. The landscape materials supply company would mix it and then they would turn around and sell it. Talk about a racket! I'm sure they made a killing on it with those double fees.

I bought tons of the stuff and had the best results with it. You need to remember that we are just talking about soil. There is a huge range of what good soil is and isn't. If you find some used soil or someone is offering you a bunch of soil for free you should take it as long as it is good soil. Your plants will love it and they don't care if it was used or free or expensive. They just want something that holds moisture and allows their roots to grow.

What you need to do before you buy your soil is to figure out how much you need. You need to know how much to get you through the first run and the season. If you are going to use pots it should be pretty easy to figure out how much soil you are going to need. First determine the volume of your pot. Next count how many you will have, then mulitiply the amount of pots by their size. This gets you how much soil you need.

Here is a quick example. We are gonna say that we have 50 pots that are 15 gallons. That means we need 750 gallons of soil. You might want to convert that to cubic yards if you buy in bulk. To do that you divide 750 gallons by 202 gallons per yard and this equals 3.7 yards of soil.

Of course you should just get four yards because you will need some extra soil for transplanting and what not. Also, they only sell it by the yard. You can never have too much potting soil.

Now, if you are using a bed to do your dep in you just need to figure out your total volume of growing area and depth. Let's say your bed is 8 feet by 40 feet by 1 foot. This means you have 320 cubic feet of soil. There are 27 cubic feet in a cubic yard. This means that you are going to need 11.85 cubic yards. Might as well round it up to 12 yards because they are gonna charge you for 12 yards.

You have determined exactly how much you need, now it is time to go shopping. Where do you get potting soil? Good locations for purchasing potting soil are landscape supply stores, nurseries, home supply centers and grow stores.

If you are on a budget you are gonna need to do a little shopping around to get the best deal. Even "cheap" soil is expensive and the price quickly adds up when you aren't looking. That's why I started using "used" soil- because it I didn't want to pay the price for the new stuff.

When you get soil delivered in bulk you will get charged for delivery. A typical delivery rate is $100 an hour. There AND back! So if it takes them an hour to get to your place it will cost $200. Soil is expensive so make sure to shop around and save yourself a buck or two.

An inexpensive way to bulk up your potting soil is to mix it with compost. Compost is usually a lot cheaper than potting soil. And it is commonly sold at the same location as the potting soil you are buying. If you are getting bulk soil delivered you can have them mix it in the same load or have them keep it separate. It's up to you.

Word of warning: DON'T plant directly into pure compost. I did it one time and burned the hell out of my plants. Compost is decayed and broken down organic matter. This means it is rich in nutrients and is essentially a fertilizer. You need to mix it with something that is inert. Then you can plant in it. When you mix it you want to use a 50/50 ratio to prevent burning. Once the nutrients from compost have been used up you basically end up with a medium grade potting soil.

Another technique to bulk up your potting soil is to mix it with your native soil. The most you want to mix in is a 50/50 ratio. This is because native soil is usually too dense. You want to break up that density so your roots can grow with ease.

There are great benefits to using native soil. Native soil is usually already teeming with beneficial microbes and it is free. That is a great price in my opinion! Native soil is usually great at retaining water which will reduce your watering work load.

If you have great native soil that is good for planting in I would still mix in some compost because even the best native soils are generally a little dense. This is just to make sure the soil is fluffier so the roots will reach out to absorb more nutrients.

When you are done you don't have to throw away your soil. You can reuse if you treat it right. In fact you can reuse your soil forever if you treat it right. Yes, even if you are using chemical fertilizers.

Treating soil properly is easy. All you need to do is if you are using chemical fertilizers is to use them in low doses and rinse the soil out with clean water when you are done with your run. There will still be a buildup of the chemicals over time but that is easily dealt with. If you let your soil get exposed to the winter rains you will be just fine. The winter rains will wash away any of your leftover salt buildup. By the time you get around to planting in the spring your soil will basically be brand new again. Of course there won't be any nutrients in the soil so you will have to fertilize again. I have used the same soil for over 10 years with this process and have great success. So, yes, it works.

Now, if you are using organic fertilizers you have nothing to worry about at all. Your soil is ready to use at all times unless you are over fertilizing. Then it may be a little hot. Just let it be exposed to the winter rains and it too will be fine.

If you have a "dead" soil and you want to revive it all you need to do is rinse it out with lots of clean water or let the winter rains take care of it for you. Then you need amend it with some organic fertilizers like Azomite and chicken shit, then you use some compost tea and plant a cover crop like alfalfa. Let the alfalfa grow for two months in the winter/spring and your soil should be good to go. It will be nice and revitalized and ready for planting.

There are only two ways to permanently kill your soil: by using an excessive amount of chemical fertilizer or using growth hormones. If you use huge amounts of chemical fertilizers there is a chance that the chemicals will bond with the soil. You could rinse it out eventually. With lots and lots of water. If you have an infinite supply of free water this is the way to go. If you don't it may be easier to replace the soil. You don't have to throw it away! You can just pile it up and let it sit outside for a couple of years and it will be ready to reuse.

If you used growth hormones your soil is pretty much fucked forever. Those chemicals seem to create a tight bond with the soil that is almost impossible to break. So you WILL need to replace the soil if you used a product with plant growth hormones in it. Basically, don't use plant growth hormones. You might get more yield for one run but you screw up your soil. You also end up with a product that you shouldn't be smoking in the first place. This will create a huge amount of work that could have been avoided.

Let's talk about Coco coir. I know it is not really considered "soil" but we use it the same way as soil. In my opinion coco is the only way to go if you are starting from scratch. It's cheap if you buy pallets of the coco blocks. When it is fully expanded with water it is fluffy, fluffy, and fluffy. The roots grow so fast through it, it's crazy! The material doesn't break down rapidly which means it is good for years of use. It will not hold an excess amount of water.

The only real drawback of using coco is it does require a lot of watering to use because it doesn't hold a lot of water. This doesn't mean you need to use excessive water. It just means that you will need to water it every day. If you have an automatic watering system this is not a problem. If you don't have an automatic watering system then you should not use coco.

18 POTS VS. BEDS

The age old debate rages on. What grows better weed: pots or beds? While there is a correct answer to the question, the correct answer largely depends on you. What is going to work better for you and the conditions you have? So we will explore the pros and cons of each in order to educate you so that you can make the best decision for your situation.

Pots
Let's start with pots and all things pots! For the sake of this exercise we are talking about black rigid plastic pots only! We are not talking about Smart Pots, cloth pots, Air-Pots or Grow Bags. While all of these are perfectly fine to grow in, we are not talking about them. We are talking about black rigid plastic pots.

First we need to consider what size pot you are going to use. There should be a minimum and a maximum size pot range for this exercise. The minimum we will consider is 10 gallons and the maximum is 30 gallons. Any smaller than that and your plants have a good chance of drying out too fast. Any larger than 30 gallons and they become too hard to move around.

Remember you are trying to grow bud, not stem. This means that you do not want to grow tall plants. Instead you want to grow wide plants. This pot size range allows you a good plant size range from small to medium sized plants.

The pot size should be able to accommodate the plant root system comfortably. This means that the roots have room to grow when planted and should max out the soil by the time harvest has arrived. If your plants are not filling up the soil in the pot by the time harvest has arrived you need a smaller pot. Or next time grow your plants a little bigger. Or plant more plants in the pot. Conversely, the opposite is true. If your plants max out the soil in the pot well before harvest you need to use a bigger pot or you need to start flowering them when they are smaller.

Ultimately you need to know that your pot size will limit your root growth potential. Your roots can not grow larger than the size of your pots; unless they are Smart Pots and the roots are growing into the ground. So if you want big plants you will need big pots.

Pots are easy to set up. You get to fill them on an individual basis. You fill them up with the amount of soil that they need, place them in a grid in the frame and you are basically done. While it does take a little extra work filling pots with a shovel, versus dumping a wheelbarrow of soil into a bed, it is still pretty easy.

Moving a pot is pretty easy, unless you have a 30 gallon pot that you have just watered. That would be a bit of a bitch. Plan on moving your pots before you water them.

Why would you want to move your plants around? When you are growing your plants you will notice that some plants grow faster than other plants. So you may have a section of plants that are tiny and another section of plants that are huge. If that is the case you can grab a few of the big plants and drag them over to the section where there are little plants and fill in the canopy. This is one of the major advantages of growing in pots. You can move your plants around without hurting them because their roots are not connected to the ground. If you are growing in a small area it is super important that you are able to move your plants around.

When it comes time to transplant into your pots it can be a bit of a bitch. Especially if you are planting one gallon pots into the above mentioned size range. Digging a hole to accommodate a one gallon pot is tricky. You need to pull out a bunch of soil so in order to fit the plant into it properly. Now you've got a hole that soil keeps falling into, so you have to dig out some more soil. So where do you put that soil? That is what you need to figure out! Just create a procedure that works for you. Whatever system you create to transplant into pots just know that it will be time consuming and labor intensive. That is just the way it is.

Your plants are safely planted and now all you need to do is water them. No problem, right? Mostly it is no problem. The only real problem is missing a pot when you water. No matter how much you try to be accurate and precise you are gonna miss a pot or two.

The best way to avoid missing a pot when you water is to create a procedure or pattern when you water. You will want to start in the same place every time and finish in the same place every time. Since each pot is an individual you need to make doubly sure that each plant gets water. So you should create an orderly system that goes up and down the line.

Setting your plants in a grid makes it a lot easier to water without missing any of the plants. If your plant layout is all over the place you are definitely more likely to miss a plant when watering. If you are unsure if you watered a plant then you should just go back and water it. You would rather accidentally water a plant twice rather than miss watering it at all.

Purchasing pots can be expensive because you are buying individual items. The bigger the pots get, the more expensive they get. Also, the bigger the pot the more expensive it becomes to fill with soil. So just make sure that you are choosing the right size pot for the project you are doing. It doesn't make good sense to waste money on something you don't need.

Beds

Beds are fairly easy to set up. You just choose the location of your bed and then you hammer some stakes into the ground. Next, you put your boards on the inside of stakes and screw the wood together. Now that you have your form you just need to fill it. If you made it easy on yourself you can just back up a dump truck and dump the soil right into the bed. If not, fill a wheel barrow and dump loads of soil into the form until it is full.

With a little bit of forethought setting up and filling a bed should be fast. There is zero mystery to it. That is one of the main reasons I like beds. You set them up and you are done with all the major work for years to come. The only "hard" work left to do is transplant into the beds.

The major drawback to using beds is the amount of soil used. You tend to use more soil when you make a bed, because you are covering more area with the soil. Instead of pinpoint locations (like a pot) you are covering everywhere. You have to consider how wide you want your bed, how long and how deep.

It is surprising how much soil it takes to fill a bed. So make sure that you are choosing the right size bed for the job at hand. For example, you don't need the bed to go all the way out to where the greenhouse plastic is. This is because your plants shouldn't be touching the plastic. When your plant rubs up against the plastic it damages the plants. You want at least a 6 inch separation between your plant and the plastic for airflow. This means your soil can be 1 to 2 feet away from the plastic. Use that rule of thumb when calculating the size of your bed and you'll save yourself a little bit of money.

Once your beds are full it is fairly easy to transplant your plants. You have all the room you need to dig. You get to choose your layout or pattern of planting. The best way is to start at one end and work your way backwards. This allows you to dig your hole as deep and as wide as you need to with a shovel! This makes for quick and easy planting when compared to transplanting into a pot.

You dig up the soil and you can place that soil anywhere because it's all soil around you. It won't be lost or spilled if you keep it in the bed. Transplanting in a bed is a breeze and if you work backwards you end up tilling the soil and making it loose and fluffy.

However, once you plant your plant that is it. There is no moving it. That is its permanent home until harvest. Once the roots have established themselves it is very unwise to try to move a plant. Especially if the plant is flowering. At this point the plant's energy focus is on creating flowers for the next generation not creating huge new root structures.

This means you really need to pay attention to which plants you plant and where you plant them. You don't want to plant a bunch of little plants together in the same spacing you planted the bigger plants. If you do you will end up with a patch that isn't filled in properly. This will lower your yield in that location.

The solution is to mix your bigger plants with you littler ones. Or if you have a bunch of little ones you should plant them all together with closer spacing. This way they will fill in the space.

Walking on your bed after it has been planted is a bad idea. Every time you walk on the bed you are stepping on the plants roots. Every time you step on the plants roots you are damaging them. This results in the plant having to repair those roots. So instead of sucking up wonderful nutrients to create more flowers the plant has to spend that energy on repairing the roots. Not only that but those damaged and broken roots will start to rot and invite in all sorts of unsavory bacteria that could infect the root zone. The message here is do not walk on the beds if you can avoid it.

Of course if you have a sick plant in the middle of the bed you should go ahead and walk in there to check it out! Get up close to see if it something you can cure or if you need to remove the plant.

Maintenance on a bed is tricky because you shouldn't walk on the bed but you need to tend your plants. This is why half of your bed width should be one arms length. This means your bed should be two of your arms lengths. This way you can reach the middle of your bed from either side.

Now, if you have more space to grow in but not enough to create two beds I recommend making your bed as big as your available space. If your space is big enough for two beds with a walkway between them then you should have two beds. The plants will grow into the walkway space so don't worry about "wasting" space.

The true benefit of growing in a bed is the space available for the roots to grow. Marijuana's ideal root zone volume for a clone is approximately 2 feet deep by as wide as they can grow in a season. That is true for a big 10 footer as well as for a 3 footer. However, most light dep plants max out at 3 feet high. So the plant roots don't really need to go 2 feet deep. On the other hand they do need to go as wide as they can as fast as the can. And that is exactly what a bed allows for. You want to allow your plants to spread their roots as wide as they can so they absorb more food. Bigger roots equal bigger plants and bigger yields.

One of the best aspects of growing in a bed is watering. Watering a bed is easier than watering pots. If you miss watering a plant that plant will probably be okay because you watered the neighbors to the east, west, south, and north of it. This means that the water will get to the missed plant by osmosis.

Let's just say you missed an entire section when you were watering. This is bad, but it is still better than using a pot because of the beds connection with the ground. The ground beneath the bed acts as sort of reservoir and holds water. It is not a large amount but it is enough to help buffer the lack of water when you fuck up.

Beds are definitely more forgiving than pots because of their ability to store water in a larger volume of soil. Even if you live in a wetter climate beds are more forgiving because you don't need to water as much.

I have seen all sorts of materials used to make beds. Pressure treated lumber, 2 by 6's, plastic lumber, plywood and even particle board! The best bang for your buck for the sidewalls is a sheet of 4 feet by 8 feet 3/8 inch plywood. Cut them into 1 foot strips that are 8 feet long. One sheet will yield 4 strips. You use this create your beds.

To make a long bed all you need to do is over lap the strips by 4 or 5 inches and screw them together. I know 3/8 inch plywood is not that thick but the pressure load on the plywood is not that great. After all, the bed is only one foot tall and no one is walking or stomping around in it. This means the plywood doesn't experience much of a load. This type of bed will last for at least 4 years, even in the weather. Don't overbuild if you don't have to is what I say.

19 OPEN AIR VS GREENHOUSE

Another great debate is open air vs greenhouse. Each has their benefits and each has their drawbacks. You need to decide which method is best for you and your pocketbook. There is no reason you couldn't use both methods at different times of the year to maximize your production. It may cost more and take more work but if you are serious about increasing your production then you need to at least consider it. Without further ado let's get into the benefits of each method.

Open Air

The open air method is exactly what it sounds like. Your plants are outside exposed to the open air. The only thing above them is the frame that you have created. This method is the most commonly used method. It is the most commonly used method for a reason: because it works.

This method is the quickest and easiest by far to set up. All you need to do is layout your frame and set it up. With minimal parts this method is essentially the cheapest to use. You could set up three frames of 10' by 100' in a day with two people! These babies are great when you are on a budget or only have a limited amount of time and human resources.

The reverse is true too. If you need to do quick teardown after the season then just using frames is the way to go. Easy up, easy down.

The open air method gives your plants great ventilation because, duh, there is nothing impeding the air flow over them. When the wind blows your plants get every little breath of fresh air. The wind will help strengthen your plants. All that fresh air helps your plants to maintain their health and vigor. For ventilation this is obviously the best method, especially in the hot summer months.

In the summer when the heat settles in you don't have to worry too much about your plants overheating. This is because there is nothing to trap the heat in. Of course if it is an extremely hot day then your plants are going to be extremely hot too because they are experiencing the ambient temperature.

On the other hand, when it is early to late spring your plants will experience the natural cold of the season. This is especially true for the early mornings which are usually the coldest times of the day. Your plants will experience the full effects of the cold. This means that during the spring your plants will be really slow to start growing in the morning because of the ambient cold. Even if it is sunny out your plants won't start production until they heat up a bit. This is effectively shortening your growing day by an hour or two because your plant has to recover from the cold before it can kick into growing gear.

Another benefit of using the open air technique is the minimization of humidity and the problems associated with humidity. Because your plants are exposed to the open air during the day there is no real threat or problem with the humidity building up on the plants. This results in your plants experiencing conditions that are far less likely to create problems such as mold or powdery mildew.

But your plants will be exposed to the morning dew. Morning dew is usually not a major concern because it evaporates slowly in the morning before it can cause problems. If for some reason your plants are infected with powdery mildew or mold then the morning dew is going to be a real problem. It will help to create ideal conditions for those problems to flourish.

The open air technique does have dangers that are associated with it. Namely the elements, rip offs and the law. When you allow your plants to be exposed to the open air you are now at the mercy of the elements. Sometimes Mother Nature will kick up a mean windstorm that will destroy your plants unless they are sheltered from the wind. I've seen this happen. You never know when the wind is going to kick up so always be prepared.

Rain can also be devastating to your plants. When your plants are young and still in the vegetative state this is not much of a problem. However, when your plants are 6 to 8 weeks into flower and a heavy rainstorm hits you could be in for some real trouble. At this stage your plants are already heavy from the bud weight and the additional water weight from the rain will break branches (even if you tied them up).

Broken branches aren't so bad. Just leave them alone if they aren't wilting. If they are wilting then harvest them. The real problem is if the plants get beat down and fall over into the ground. Now you have bud that is covered in dirt. It happens! If this happens to you get a bucket of water, submerge the dirty buds and shake until they come clean. What a pain in the ass!

The open air method should only be used if you have privacy. If you are in a crowded neighborhood you do not want to use this technique because you could encourage rip offs. Sad but true. Another concern of course is Johnny Law. The law has access to the eyes in the sky and will be able to spot your light dep garden easily. Without a cover they will have no problem spotting exactly what you are growing. This could lead to a personal visit from your local neighborhood law enforcement team.

If you are only using the open air method and nothing else you will be limited to two harvests max per year. This is assuming you are not doing any light breaking. And even if you are doing light breaking it would still be hard to achieve more than two harvests because of the cold temperatures in the spring. Those cold temps will really slow your plant's growth to a crawl.

Now if you live in a warmer climate like southern California or southern Texas you could definitely pull off more than two harvests per season. You just need a warm climate and a good plan that is detailed about start and end times.

Greenhouse

Depping in a greenhouse is completely different than depping in the open air. Well, not really, but you do have a lot more things that you need to pay attention to. First you need to determine if you are going to have an internal frame or are you going to pull your blackout plastic over the greenhouse plastic.

Both are effective and work quite well, but an internal frame is easier to pull the plastic over. Of course you need a big enough greenhouse to build an internal frame. An internal frame is the same as the frame you build outside except you build it inside the greenhouse.

If you have small greenhouse it will be easier to just pull the blackout plastic over the greenhouse itself. Just a word of warning: when you pull the blackout plastic over the greenhouse plastic there will be a huge amount of friction. This means that is will be a lot harder to pull the plastic over your frame. It can be done. People do it all the time. Just yank away!

When you dep using a greenhouse it is typically called "black box." If you have heard this term and wondered what it means this is it. Some people will tell you that it is different than depping outside and it is. But only because it is done in a greenhouse.

Depping in a greenhouse offers many benefits. You will be able to yield more bud faster and earlier. How you ask? Well, first you get to start your plants earlier outside with light breaking of course. Since your plants are in a greenhouse they will be able to better withstand the cold spring (if you live in a colder climate). Not only will your plants be able to withstand the cold spring- they will thrive. The warmth the greenhouse provides will keep the plants and roots warmer allowing the roots to actively grow. Roots don't grow so well below 60 degrees Fahrenheit.

With your starts growing in spring you will be able to get the plants bigger at a faster rate. So when it comes time to start pulling your tarps you won't have to wait around for your plants to grow and fill in the space.

Bigger plants faster = more weed! That's not rocket science- just plain old facts. Thanks greenhouse! Seriously, if you start in early spring on growing your plants you will be able to pull off three harvests in one season with the right planning.

The greenhouse plastic acts as a barrier to the elements. The plastic will capture the heat and trap it inside with the plants. Thus keeping them nice and cozy in the spring and fall. Not only does the plastic capture the sun's heat it will also protect your plants from the wind. The wind can be a nasty foe.

The wind in spring will whip around and potentially destroy your plants. Not only that, but the wind rips away the heat from your plants. If you don't believe me go ahead and stand outside on windy spring day with no jacket. You'll get cold quick. Then go and find a spot that is just as sunny as the windy spot but is sheltered from the wind. I bet you'll find that it is a lot warmer. You need the greenhouse to protect your plants from the cold spring wind.

Not to mention cold rain. Cold rain will slow your growth tremendously with a slight chance of overwatering your plants as well. Growth really slows down on a rainy day because of the cloudy sky. On a rainy spring day your plants are receiving half the amount of light they would normally get. They are cold because there is no sun out AND they are soaking wet. Not what I would call ideal conditions.

With a greenhouse to protect your plants from the elements in fall you will be able to plant that last run a little later and be able to harvest a little bit later. Your plants will continue to grow well into November without all the problems that come with being outside. No cold, no wind, and no rain. This means you will be able to let your plants finish when they are supposed to instead of cutting them down early because of lousy conditions.

You know what else a greenhouse protects your plants from? Deer. Have you ever seen a garden that has been grazed over by deer? They are really effective at pruning! You really only have to worry about deer when your plants are in the vegetative state. Apparently they taste yummy at that stage. Once your plants are into full blooming stage they are less than appealing to deer. But during that small window when your plants are vegging out you are particularly vulnerable to deer. One deer can decimate a dep garden in a matter of minutes. So again… thank your greenhouse for its protection.

Not everything is peaches and cream when using a greenhouse. There are a lot of potential problems that need to be addressed in order to have a satisfactory outcome. In spring you don't need to worry about heat- in fact you are trying to capture the heat.

In the summer months and early fall you are trying to get rid of the heat. Remember you are trying to keep your plants in the sweet zone of 70 to 85 degrees Fahrenheit or at least the ambient temperature outside. Now in the summer months it can be 80 degrees outside and 110 degrees inside your greenhouse. This is a MASSIVE problem that needs to be addressed before it becomes a problem. You need to open the ends and sides of your greenhouse to allow airflow through the greenhouse. You will also need to vent using fans or vent through the peak of your greenhouse.

Can you imagine what the temperatures would be like in the greenhouse if it is 100 degrees outside? Sweltering. Those kinds of temperatures will STOP your plants from growing. Period. So you will end up with less than half of what you should have produced.

With soaring temperatures and a protected environment you have also left yourself open to pest infestation. Talk about great conditions for spider mites! I have seen a greenhouse that was unvented get taken over by mites in a matter of 2 weeks.

What I'm saying is vent, vent, vent!!! Remove the heat as best you can when it gets over 85 degrees.

The great news is all of those problems can be addressed with effort and some money. The real great news is you can harvest at least three times a year if you use a greenhouse in your operation. If you are really ambitious you can harvest five times a year. Now, if you are going to harvest five times a year you will need to use lights and all sorts of stuff. That is a subject for another book!

Something to consider when light depping is the privacy that using a greenhouse affords you. The plastic sheeting for greenhouse is usually opaque. This means it lets the light in while blocking sight of what is actually inside the greenhouse.

Of course everyone already knows what is inside the greenhouse but do they REALLY know? That little bit of doubt, believe it or not, really protects the gardener. It protects you from rip-offs and it protects you from the law. The law cannot search your property if they can't see your plants. So if everything on your property is in compliance then the cops will have no probable cause to search your property. While it is not a huge amount of protection at least it is something. And every little bit counts when you are growing weed.

20 PLANT DENSITY & CREATING THE CANOPY

To make sure you are making the most of the sunlight the spacing of your plants is very important. The spacing you choose is dependent on the variety of your plants and their size. For the sake of argument we will say that there are two types of plants: 8 weekers and 10 weekers. Let's briefly go over their characteristics that apply to spacing.

8 weekers tend to be shorter and they also tend to trigger quicker into flowering. This means that they will not stretch and grow much once flowering has started.

10 weekers tend to be lanky and they also tend to trigger slowly into flowering. This means that they will stretch and grow once flowering has started.

Knowing these characteristics is key in deciding what kind of spacing you are going to use when you plant your plants. This applies to pots as well as beds. For pots you get a little more leeway because you can move them around and with beds you need to be more precise because you can't move them around.

If you are using 8 weekers you will want them to be planted or laid out closer to each other because they don't stretch too much.

On the other hand if you are using 10 weekers you will want to make sure that when you plant them that they get a little more room to grow because they are going to stretch out.

In my humble opinion it is best to lay out your plants in a grid for their final location. This allows you to perform maintenance and keep track of them in a systematic order. This is a huge boon when you are dealing with lots of plants.

The true goal is to fill in your canopy. Not as full as possible, because you can grow your plants huge and call that a canopy. That is not at all what I'm talking about. Let me define what I consider "The Canopy."

This definition for the canopy only applies to light dep. It does not apply to growing big plants or growing indoors. This is only for light dep. Here is the ideal canopy that you are trying to achieve: You want to fill all the space as if it is a hedge, where the plants are touching but not too much. The canopy extends down 18 to 24 inches. This means you can have plant material 18 to 24 inches below the top of the canopy. Any deeper than this and you are wasting your plant's energy because the buds below aren't receiving enough light to grow. This means they are diverting your plants energy from growing bud into growing squaff. Squaff is tiny airy bud that no one wants.

So you want your canopy to be 18 to 24 inches deep and your plants touching up top. It should look a lot like a hedge. Of course you don't want your canopy to be too dense up top because you need some light penetration below to activate the lower buds.

When you properly fill your canopy you will produce more bud, bottom line.

In order for you to fill your canopy in a timely manner you need to figure out how many plants you are going to need. You are going to have to ask yourself some questions first. Such as: do you want to grow bigger plants or do you want to grow littler plants? Once you have determined that it becomes a lot easier to determine how many plants you will need to grow.

Now you need to figure out the size of the area you are growing in. This is easy. All you need to do to determine the area is measure the length and the width. Multiply them together and you have your area. You still need to determine how many plants you need but you are most of the way there.

I am going to go over two examples with the same size area. One example will be with bigger plants and the other example will be with smaller plants. The area we are going to use is a 10' by 10' space. This is equal to 100 square feet.

Example 1.

A bigger plant for light dep is usually 2 feet in diameter. This means you can plant 5 rows by 5 columns. This equals 25 plants that will fit in the area. But wait a minute your plants are round and I calculated them as if they were square! I know, I know. You have two options. Option 1 let them grow a little and fill in the space or Option 2 plant a few extra in the vacant space. I have found that it is usually better to let them fill in on their own but the decision is yours.

Example 2.

A smaller plant for light dep is usually 1 foot in diameter. This means you can plant 10 rows by 10 columns. This equals 100 plants. The same thing applies here as the other example.

When using small plants you end up using a lot more of them! I recommend getting started a little earlier and getting them a little bigger.

Remember, these are just examples. There are many ways to tackle this problem. I have seen big ass plants in a dep and I have seen tiny plants too. Just figure out what you want to end up with size wise and calculate backwards to arrive at how many plants you will need.

ALWAYS start with more plants than you think you need!

So you determined how many plants you need and now you are ready to plant. You grew a bunch extra just in case and now you need to choose which plants to plant.

Obviously you want to choose only the healthy and vigorous plants. Leave the sick or stunted ones to the side. You may be able to nurse them back to health later. DON'T PLANT THE SICK ONES IN YOUR DEP!!! They may come around later but right now they are sick and need to be babied. You only want healthy plants in the dep. Remember they only have 8 to 10 weeks to do their thing so they need to be healthy!

Now that you have chosen the healthy ones, it is time to choose plants based on size. Here are a couple rules of thumb: keep the same size plants together and plant the tall ones on the north side. If you keep the same size together they will create a uniform canopy which is great. A uniform canopy is easier to work with and a more efficient use of the available sunlight.

If your plants are all over the place size wise you can prune the taller ones so that they are approximately the same size as the smaller ones. This is a technique that I have used on more than one occasion. A word of warning: prune you plants AT LEAST a week before you start depping. This ensures that you won't stunt your plant's growth.

Always plant your tallest plants as far from the sun's path as possible. This way when they grow even taller they won't shade out the shorter plants.

Another choice to make: monocropping or multiple varieties?

Monocropping is when you plant all the same variety. For example, you only plant Trainwreck and just Trainwreck. That is monocropping and it has many advantages. When you monocrop you know all the plants are going to finish at the same time because they are all the same variety. They will also grow at the same rate and fill in at the same rate. This makes it easy to determine exactly how big your plants are going to grow if you are familiar with the plant and its growth rate.

A major problem with monocropping is the plant's susceptibility. If the variety you choose is susceptible to mold that means the whole light dep is susceptible to mold. This is not a cause for alarm it is just a cause for concern. If you are paying attention to your plants with the proper maintenance you will have no problems whatsoever.

You may choose to plant **multiple varieties** when you do your light dep. I have done it with great success and you can too. However, I must caution on a few things that you need to pay attention to such as: grouping your varieties together and harvest times.

When you are doing more than one variety in a dep you always want to group them together. You should do this for a couple of reasons. Since they are the same variety they will likely grow at the same rate. This way you know how your canopy will fill in. Secondly you want to be able to keep track of varieties when you harvest. You don't want to be mixing your OG's with your Blue Dreams. I know you can tell them apart! But can your worker? And if they can, will they keep it separate? Maybe.

The most important reason to keep varieties together is because they finish at the same time. Can you imagine the extra work that you would need to do if you have different varieties randomly planted together? You have to harvest these five, but not that one because it has two weeks to go. Never mind that the trellising is wrapped around everything. Been there, done that. Lesson learned.

Which brings me to my next point, you should only plant 8 weekers with 8 weekers and you should only plant 10 weekers with 10 weekers. This just makes harvesting a lot easier and decreases your workload.

The real kicker about not mixing them is you may be tempted to replant after the 8 weekers are done and the 10 weekers have two weeks left. The problem with that is your 10 weekers may be infected with something that they just casually pass on to your new crop. It just isn't worth the risk in my opinion.

Of course, if you only have enough plants to fill the space and it's a mixed bag you should definitely mix the 8 and 10 weekers together. There almost always is an exception to every rule.

Which is worse too dense or too sparse? Well, this comes down to the bottom line. If your canopy is too sparse you must wait until it fills in before covering. Otherwise you will not produce the yield that you desire. It may take a week to fill in or may take a month to fill in. Either way it is unwise to start covering before it is time.

If your canopy is too dense that can be a real problem. A canopy that is too dense lends itself to all sorts of potential diseases. It will also lead to a subpar yield because of all the wasted energy the plant is spending on trying to build buds that are shaded out.

The good news is it is a very simple problem to solve. Just bust out your pruners and get to work. You are going to need to be an Edward Scissorhands on you canopy. Don't be shy about trimming your plants back. They are very hardy and re-grow quickly. If you don't cut them back enough you'll just end up back in there doing it again in two weeks.

If you are inexperienced at how much to cut back you will need to do an experiment for your own education. The experiment goes like this: create three sections that you are going to trim. A small section that you will trim back HARD, a small section that you will trim back lightly, and a big section where you trim the plants back the way you think they should be done.

After two weeks go back and check on those sections and trim them again if you need to. I bet you will find that you will need to trim all three sections again. Of course the section that you trimmed back hard will need the least amount of trimming and the other two will seem like you didn't even bother to trim in the first place.

As an inexperienced grower you will probably need to repeat this experience a few times before you really get the hang of it. But you will and then you'll be able to save yourself a lot of work and frustration.

Another skill that develops with time is the ability to fill the canopy just right and on schedule. This is not something that just happens by accident. You will need to learn exactly how fast your variety grows given the conditions that you are giving them. Don't be crestfallen if you don't nail it exactly right the first couple of go rounds. This will take time for you to get a sense of how fast it takes your plants to grow at certain times of the year. How fast they grow in the pots they are in. There are several little details that you will learn to pay attention to over time. Be patient and take notes. Trust me, your memory ain't that great!

The true secret here is to stick to one or two varieties and learn the ins and outs. Once you have that down you will know without a doubt how to proceed. By knowing and mastering your variety of choice you will be able to accurately predict the plant's growth rate during vegetative growth, during preflower, and during budding. Knowing all these phases will give you an edge on pulling off the season of a lifetime. Believe me it is all in the details. Or as they say "the devil is in the details." And boy are they right!

Sometimes you'll end up on the short end of the stick when it comes to having enough plants. If you end up not having enough plants you will just have to let them grow to fill in the space. The best way to do that is to pinch the tops so that your plant grows laterally versus vertically. You know, sideways versus tall.

Another technique that works very well for filling in an area with one plant is to bend your plant over as it grows. If you continually tie your plant down once a week you will be surprised at how much area your plant can cover. I have seen one plant that was 13 feet in diameter. I have also been told by a reliable source that he grew a plant that was 18 feet in diameter and it yielded 13 pounds of smoke! That is some incredible shit right there!

As your plants grow you will have to water more often because bigger plants need more water then little plants. Nothing magical about that but you need to remember to increase your frequency of watering if you want to sustain the growth rate.

Making use of all your space is very important to achieve the results that you want. To make the best use of all your space will take some great planning, a great layout and time.

Taking the time to plan out your strategy to make the best use of your space is time well spent. The planning is so instrumental in going forward, because it gives you an objective that will be easier to achieve because you won't be wasting your time on the age old question of "what's next?" You'll know the answer already and go about achieving it.

Choosing the correct layout for your space is also important. With the right layout you will be able to fill your canopy with the minimum amount of plants instead of just having to pack in a ton of extra and unnecessary plants. If you do the correct layout you will save yourself a ton of work because you won't have to grow extra plants, and plant extra plants, and water extra plants and…..

So take the time to figure out exactly what you need and how to go about getting it done so you only need to do it once. Instead of redoing it and then redoing it again. Been there done that. Lame.

You may be wondering if having tall plants versus short plants is better. The truth is they are both great methods. All you need to do is figure out which one you would like to grow.

Traditionally tall plants are wider so you end up having less plants but they take longer to grow to size. Short plants cover a smaller area and you end up using more plants to fill in the space. You just need to decide which is the best method for you and your time.

Your canopy must be kept within the bounds of your light dep. Do not let your plants grow so big that they are touching the ribs or the plastic when it is pulled over. This will damage your plants. And damaged plants don't produce as much as healthy plants on average.

If your canopy is growing into the ribs or plastic you need to tie them down or away from the plastic. This can be a bit of a bitch if you have a dense canopy. But you can do it, I believe in you. One of the things that I do is bend a branch over until it gets a kink in it. I know this sounds brutal- it is. But that is okay because the branch will continue to grow and produce great bud. Now, I am not advocating this method as a way to deal with your whole canopy. I only use this method if the plant is running into the plastic AND there is nothing to easily tie it down with.

Always consider ease of access when you are creating your layout, plant density and canopy density. You must be able to maintenance your garden at all phases. While it may be true that you won't have to do any real maintenance during the flowering cycle you must plan as if you will need to.

I guarantee that if you don't create access to your plants that you will run into problems because you will need to maintenance them. Of course the opposite is true. If you provide access somehow you won't need to do any maintenance. That is Murphy's Law. Damn Murphy.

Either way you will need to be able to reach into the canopy to water. I know you have an automatic watering system but sometimes that shit fails and you need to be prepared to water by hand. Hell, you will probably need to gain access to your canopy after 2-3 weeks of flowering to deleaf or prune out the undergrowth.

Make your life a little easier and plan a method that will provide you access to your canopy.

21 HARVEST

Harvest is everyone's favorite time of the run. You've put in the hard work and now you get a chance to reap the benefits. Well I got news for you, it ain't over yet. You can still fuck up. I have watched this time and again. People get it in their heads that they have already done all the hard work and now they can relax.

This is so far removed from the truth that I need to warn you. I have seen tragedies during harvest that will make you want to cry. Here are a few examples of harvesting tragedies…

-I once watched someone harvest and hang their plants up to dry. And he let it mold because he thought it would "just take care of itself."

-One gentleman set up a dry room and used heaters on both ends, with no fans and ended up with mold in the middle.

-One time I saw someone wait and wait and wait to harvest because he wanted them to put on more weight and he lost half his crop due to mold.

I saved the worst for last. One time I watched a guy burn down his dry shed on accident. What's worse than that? He did it again less than a month later! FUCK!!!!!!! I mean FUCK!!!!!!!!

Enough of the scare tactics let's get down to the serious business of harvesting. The best time to harvest is when your crop is ripe or they are in serious danger of a plague of some sort (mold, fire, police, frost…) AND there is something worth harvesting.

The common practice is when 50% of the white hairs on each plant turn brown. That is a good general indicator. No doubt about it. Just go out to your garden and take a look around. If there are hairs that are half brown it is a good time to take them.

When growing light dep we are on a tight schedule. Just because we are on a schedule doesn't mean you should harvest because your calendar says "harvest day is such and such." If your plants are premature DON'T harvest. Wait the additional week or two. You will be well rewarded. Be patient.

On the other hand, if your plants have finished a little early and your next wave of plants aren't ready then wait a little to harvest, they will put on a little more weight and crystals. If you aren't in a rush wait a little. Now if your next wave of plants are ready and your plants finished a little early, harvest that shit! Get your next wave in the ground and let them get a head start on establishing their roots.

Your harvesting method depends upon a lot of variables. Such as uniformity of crop. Was everything planted at the same time? Are there problems that need to be addressed?

Ideally you have chosen a strain or two that harvest at the same time. If this is the case, and I hope it is, you can harvest everything at once. This should be your goal, to harvest everything at once. It makes everything simple and streamlines the process. When you do a mass harvest you are less likely to forget a crucial part of the process. You will also be able to get more work done in a day then if you have to selectively harvest. When you do the same job all day you get fast and efficient at it. When you skip around and work over here, then over here, then over there, you waste a lot time. Lastly when you harvest all at once you are physically removing any problems or potential problems that may have lived on or in the plant.

When you have problems in the garden it is okay to selectively harvest. If a plant needs to go because of some problem, it needs to go. Don't wait to see if it gets better, it probably won't and the sun will actually damage it. Protect what bud you can, while you can.

Depending on the quantity or size of your harvest you may want a dedicated room to dry your bud. If you have a small harvest that you can dry in a closet, you should dry it in the closet. Don't set up a room if you don't need to. It would be a waste of money and time. You know how I feel about wasting time and money.

Now, if you are going to have a big quantity to harvest and dry it is definitely worth dedicating a room to dry in. With a dedicated room you will be able to control access to the room as well as control all the environmental aspects of the room. Controlling who goes in and out is important for peace of mind as well as safety. Safety for you, for others, and for your bud! A dedicated room also makes it easier to work because you will have room to maneuver.

Controlling the environment in your dry room is sooooo important that it can't be overstated. This is the phase where if something goes wrong you can't just add a little water and the plants will perk right up. They are dead at this point and you need to care for every aspect that the bud needs. This is not the time to slack off.

Setting Up Your Dry Room

Setting up your dry room needs some forethought. Not a lot, granted, but it does need some. The things you want to consider are ease of use, ease of access, how many levels and where you are going to set up your lines.

First you need to determine where you are going to set up the lines that you are going to hang the plants from. If you are not familiar with this lingo, let me explain. You will string up wire from one side of the room to the other to hang your plants on upside down.

The fastest way to do this is to screw a 2x4 the length of the wall at the height you want. Make sure to screw it into the studs of course! Now go to the opposite wall and do the same thing. On those 2x4's you need to screw in some 2 inch wood screws into the top with ½ inch of the screw sticking up. The screws should be placed 12 to 18 inches apart. Next you need some bailing wire or some heavy duty wire to attach to the screws. You start at the first screw and securely attach the wire to it by wrapping it around several times. Now take the wire across the room and attach it to the corresponding first screw on the other side. Repeat this until you are done. If you decided on using two levels then you do the same thing with one level high and one level lower. Of course, you should do the higher level first for ease of installation.

Sealing your room from the outside world is a good idea. When you are sealed off you have better control of the room and better control usually means a better cure. Which is what we are after. The outside world is an amazing place, no doubt. But when it comes to drying and curing your bud it is not. The outside conditions change too fast and may not be favorable in the first place to drying your bud.

In my opinion your room should definitely be sealed. Just for safety sake. Now, if you are of the mind that you want to have some ventilation in your dry room keep in mind that you want to dry out the air inside the dry room. When you dry out the air in the dry room the plant responds by releasing moisture into the air to achieve a balance. The balance is achieved when the moisture inside the plant is equal to that of the moisture in the air. Now if you keep bringing in fresh air, how are you going to achieve that sort of static equilibrium? You really can't because the outside world is always changing. There are an exceptions of course (isn't there always?). If it is summer and constantly dry you could use this to your advantage- but only use open air ventilation if you are an experienced grower.

Hanging Your Plants

When you harvest your plants and bring the plants to the already set up dry room it's time to start hanging them up. The best way to hang them up is upside down. By hanging them upside down all the leaves will sag due to gravity to the top of the plant. This is actually a technique that protects the bud from harm.

The leaves will sort of wrap themselves around the bud in the drying process. These leaves act as a shield or buffer from getting damaged by outside forces (e.g. humans). This small protection shield helps to keep the beauty and crystals on the bud intact.

Hanging the plants upside down also helps to shape the bud into a tighter bud because the branches and bud tend to collapse inwards instead of outwards. If you hung them up right side up the bud would open up and not look too pretty. It would be a bitch to trim too!

When you are hanging your plants up space them on the line so that they are barely touching each other if they are on the same line. This will allow them to dry evenly. However, if you have a bunch of weed to hang it is okay to stuff them in there tightly. As long as you have adequate air flow you will be just fine.

Dry Room Temperature & Humidity

The best temperature range to keep your drying room is under 80 degrees Fahrenheit. Most people will tell you that keeping your dry room warm is a great idea. A warm room does speed up the drying process because the warmer the air is the more moisture the air can hold. The truth is the absolute best cure takes place in a cool dry place. 60 degrees Fahrenheit is far better for your bud then 80 degrees Fahrenheit as long as the air is *dry*. The cooler temperature may slow the process down because of the air's ability to hold less moisture, but if you add a few fans and have air whipping gently around, your plants will dry just fine.

You really do want a lot of air movement in your dry room. This allows you to substantially increase the rate at which your plants will dry. The air movement should be able to penetrate through to every hanging plant on every line. This does not mean that the air should be able to go through the plant. The wind should just be able to flow across every hanging plant. This will allow the moisture that is trapped inside the plant to flow out in a gentle manner.

How much air is too much and how much is enough? If you have so much air flow that you are damaging your drying bud then you have too much air in that location. You should never damage your bud with wind. Just relocate the fan or move the bud around. The right amount of air flow is achieved when everything that is hanging gets touched just a little by the breeze. All you need is a gentle breeze.

I bet you are wondering what happens if your dry room gets too hot. It is all sorts of bad.

You basically will lose a lot of value overnight. How? Smell, that's how. The smell in marijuana is highly sensitive to temperature. If your room gets too hot the smell in your plants will volatize (evaporate) into the air. You will basically lose all that delicious smell because your room got too hot for too long. Just try to keep your room below 80 degrees Fahrenheit and you'll be fine.

Now in the cold months you will be tempted to add a heat source in your dry room. Just a couple of words on that… if you do add a heat source you need to be cautiously alarmed. You NEED TO SECURE YOUR HEATER SO IT CAN'T FALL OVER AND BURN THE PLACE DOWN. You also need to make sure that your hanging plants are AT LEAST 3 FEET AWAY FROM THE HEAT SOURCE OR YOU COULD BURN THE PLACE DOWN.

Lastly, if you are adding an unvented propane heater you need to be aware that you are adding water to the air.

The reaction goes something like this:

PROPANE + OXYGEN transforms to HEAT + CO_2 + WATER

This is fine as long as you are aware of it and a have a plan to deal with it- such as drying out the air. If you don't dry out the air you are going to have a real problem. Namely mold.

Humidity is the moisture content in the air. When you read a humidity meter they are called relative humidity readings. Now, as I said before, there is a direct relationship between humidity and temperature. Namely the higher the temperature, the more moisture the air can hold and the lower the temperature, the less moisture the air can hold.

This does not mean that at colder temperatures you can't dry your weed. This just means that at colder temperatures that air is able to hold less moisture. This means you need to remove the moisture from the air at a faster rate.

The target humidity when you are drying your weed is between 30% and 40% humidity. This is a humidity range that will dry out your bud in a reasonable speed without compromising quality.

When your plants are fully dry your target range changes a little bit. When your bud is dry you want your humidity to be around 40%. This will keep you bud nice and stable without being too dry or too wet.

If your bud is too dry it will get crispy and fall apart when you pull it off the line or when you trim it. Not good. If it is too wet it could start to mold and wet weed is really hard to trim. So try to get your weed to 40% when it's done drying.

I'm sure you already figured out how to dry your bud by using a dehumidifier. This is the way most people do their drying and I recommend this method because it's proven and it works. You just put a dehumidifier in the room and set it to 35% humidity and come back and empty the bucket regularly or set up a hose that drains the bucket.

Now this is super important: You should only use a dehumidifier in a SEALED room. If you are venting while using a dehumidifier then you are wasting your time and money because you will just keep bringing in fresh air that you have to remove the moisture from. Don't do this. Please don't do this! You could end up allowing your weed to mold because it isn't getting dry. Just seal the room already!

The best part of a dehumidifier is the control you get to exert over your drying times and process. If you want to do it fast you can and if you want to do it slow you can. I love dehums and you should too.

With all this technology available to us the temptation is to dry our stuff fast. We are a society that wants what it wants and wants it NOW! Don't fall into this trap. Let your weed dry slowly so that it can preserve all the best qualities it can. Like I said already, the plant is dead at this point and what is in it, is in it. You can't put anything back into it. All you can do at this point is take stuff away. So just take away the moisture and preserve everything else. The way to do that is to dry your plants SLOWLY.

In this case slowly is 6 to 7 days. When you think about it, that is still pretty fast. You harvest and a week later it is dry, ready to be trimmed and smoked!

If you dry it any faster than 6 to 7 days you have the potential to damage it. If you let it take longer you are exposing it to excess moisture over a prolonged period of time which could lead to rotting and mold.

Now it is true these conditions also hold true for the 6 to 7 day window, but in my experience this window is the best compromise between too short and too long.

So how do you tell if it is done? Well I'll tell you NOT how to do it. I have seen beginners do this time and again so pay attention. You check out the plant and notice the outside leaves are nice and crispy. The bud is a little crispy too. Oh shit, you over dried it! Let's bag it up before it gets too dry! Whew, we just avoided disaster! Now let's start trimming tomorrow. But you pull out the weed and it's all wet! How did that happen? You could have sworn it was dry!

I have seen this happen a bunch of times, so let this be a lesson to you. The worst case scenario is when you think it's dry, bag it up and wait a week or two to start trimming. You open the bag and all you find is moldy ass bud!

You need to learn how to tell if your weed is actually dry. The outside layer of the plant will always dry first because it is exposed to the dry air. The plant dries from the outside in! Not the other way around.

This is how you check to see if your weed is really dry. Find a water leaf and grab it by the end and pull it up. If it snaps where it meets the stalk there is a good chance that it might be dry. If it just bends it is wet and needs to dry more. That was test number 1. Test number 2 is to grab the main stalk of that plant you just tested and see if it will snap when you bend it. If it does, then it is dry. If it bends then it is wet and needs to dry more.

Now when you run these tests you need to check all around the room not just the perimeter. You really need to check the plants on the interior, because if they are dry, then all the plants are dry.

After you have bagged up your weed you need to keep the tops open for a few days with the dehum running just in case you accidentally bagged up some wet weed. This will give the moisture a chance to evaporate out without molding the entire bag.

Here a couple of quick drying guidelines: Your temperature should not exceed 80 degrees Fahrenheit, your humidity target range is between 30-40%, make sure you have adequate air flow, use dehumidifiers, make TRIPLE sure your weed is dry before you bag it up and lastly NEVER ADD WET WEED (FRESHLY HARVESTED) TO YOUR DRYING ROOM WHEN YOUR PLANTS THAT ARE IN THERE ARE ALMOST DONE! This causes your dry weed to get wet all over again and now you have to wait until it dries out again! While it's not a huge deal if you need the space to hang more weed it can become a serious problem. Just finish each wave completely before adding new weed to the room.

22 HIRING HELP

If you do decide to hire someone you need to have very strict guidelines to follow. You should make a list of criteria that you use to hire someone. Need I say the most important criteria is reliability? I thought not.

Don't hire someone who has proven themselves to be unreliable in the past. This isn't Mr. Fixit. This is light dep! You ain't fixing anyone, nor should you try. I know it's tempting to help a friend out who is down and out. There is a reason that they are down and out. I'm not saying don't help your friend. What I'm saying is don't hire him or her to be in charge of your dep.

As a great friend of mine said to me once, "James you are on a losing streak and you aren't about to quit are you!" Notice it was a statement and not a question. Well he was right about that! During that period of my life I was on a self induced losing streak and I was committed to it. Time passed and I got over it. But during that particular time period I wouldn't have hired me either. The point is you know when your friends are on that losing streak and the worst thing you could do to yourself is to hire them! Help them all you want- just don't count on them to get the job done because they won't. Or worse they'll bring their problems home to you. That case is so much worse than them not being dependable!

Don't try to drag people along to success. Instead find someone who wants to be successful and use the hell out of them! That sounds bad but it doesn't have to be. If you do use the hell out of them you will be more successful and they'll be more successful as well. They will learn tons of useful information that they can use in the future to secure their financial freedom and at the same time they are getting paid to learn. It really is a win-win situation.

Don't hire drama queens because you will be the next source of their endless drama! Fucking drama queens! If someone is a drama queen they are always going to act like a drama queen. Remember that. They are not going to make an exception for you. This is who they are. They do make great friends, but they make shitty employees.

Let me repeat: don't hire someone who isn't enthusiastic or someone who has proven themselves to be unreliable. You shouldn't have to try to drag someone to success. When you try to do that all you are really doing is slowing yourself down. You don't need that kind of nonsense in your life. You deserve better and I am here to remind you of that.

When you hire someone you need to first determine what you are okay with and what you aren't okay with. Make a list of exactly what you expect out of your employee. The more detailed the list the better. Not just for you but for them as well. You cannot expect your worker to know everything, nor should they. They are just a worker. The only way to expect more out of them is if they are an experienced grower and getting paid really well or they are a business partner.

If your assistant is there for just two days a week I suggest you have them only do two things besides cover. Do some light clean up around the place and water. Of course watering should take priority! Anymore than that and I have found that they get resentful. Besides do you really want to trust your garden to someone who is unsupervised and doesn't have a vested interest? The answer is NO! No, you do not! Just have them cover and water and you should be golden.

Unsupervised help is a major no-no. I have suffered too much because of this. The sad part is it was entirely my fault. The fault was mine because of miscommunications on my part or expecting unrealistic objectives. When you tell someone to do something, you need to understand that they don't hear what you said. They hear something else entirely. I just mean that if there are two ways to interpret what you said I guarantee they heard it the other way. If you don't believe me go tell someone something that is mildly complex and have them repeat what you just said. I bet 9 times out of 10 you get something back you didn't intend.

You are not as effective at communicating as you thought. No one is. And if someone misinterprets what you said is it their fault or yours? The truth is it doesn't matter because your plants are fucked! That's all that matters.

So unsupervised help is a no-no unless your worker is experienced!

Make sure that you have a back up worker or two because life happens and if you don't plan for it you are going to get screwed. Enough said I think.

Another option for covering when you aren't there is buying an auto light dep machine. Yes they are reliable and work real well. I'll cover them in another chapter.

If you know you have a planned trip during the middle of your run you need to make sure that your shit is covered. You may need to beg borrow and plead to get someone to do it for you. If that is what you have to do then that is what you have to do.

If you can't get someone to cover it while you are away you may need to reschedule your trip or cancel it altogether. Hey, life ain't fair! Get over it. Life will seem fair when you harvest I guarantee it!

Honestly, if you can't reschedule your trip and you can't get someone to cover you are better off delaying your start time because of all the potential disasters of interrupting your light schedule. That or buy an Auto Light Dep Greenhouse or retrofit kit from my business Humboldt Light Dep Company (humboldtlightdep.com). Your choice.

23 PLANNING AHEAD & PROBLEM SOLVING

Disasters happen. It is the way of the world. There is no plan that is foolproof because you cannot completely control your environment. You will always be under the sway of outside influence. The sooner that you accept this, the sooner you can get to developing your own plans for disasters.

The good news is you can develop a plan to handle just about any disaster that may come your way. When you develop a good plan for a particular disaster you stand a great chance of minimizing the effects of that disaster. This is why you should develop plans for possible disasters. So in case something bad does happen you will be able to save the day and instead of losing everything you only lose a much smaller percentage.

Of course there are some scenarios that can happen that are 100% inevitable. Try as you might the event is just going to happen. For those events there is nothing you can do and shouldn't waste your time thinking about them too much.

Obviously if a disaster is preventable you want to take every preventable step before it does become a disaster. But sometimes life gets away from you and BAM the next thing you know your garden is half dead because of it.

What you need to do is develop a procedure to create disaster plans. Sounds a bit wacky, "make a plan to make plans!" but this exact method has saved my bacon on more than one occasion. If you have been reading this book you will notice that I have fucked up left, right, and center on more than one occasion- and I learned from each fuck up.

You don't get to where I'm at without developing skills to offset problems. The first thing you need to do is learn about every potential disaster out there. Of course I'm kidding- to a degree. You do need to learn about as many different kinds of disasters that usually happen to a weed grower. The best way to do this is to ask fellow growers what kinds of problems they have experienced. Reading weed forums on the internet and grow books are also a great source of information. I feel like this book has been chock full of disasters to avoid. Another great source is talking to your local grow shop. They get to hear all sorts of stupid that can be avoided. Plus it is quite entertaining to listen to.

Now I want you to make a list of all the types of disasters that you have learned about. Yes I'm serious. This list will end up saving YOUR BACON in the future. Once you have your list of disasters you need to find out how to prevent them from happening in the first place. After you learned how to prevent them from happening it is time to learn how to deal with them once they happen. Unfortunately I can promise you that at least one of the disasters on your list will happen to you. So it is in your best interest to know how to deal with it before it becomes an unstoppable disaster.

The side effect of learning about disasters and how to deal with them develops sound knowledge of how to grow excellent weed. Another side effect is your base of knowledge will be so great that if some kind of new disaster strikes that is not on your list you will more than likely be able to handle it because of the knowledge in your head.

That is an irreplaceable learned skill that every weed grower wishes they had. This learned skill won't happen overnight but I can promise you that once you develop it you will be able to grow the best bud out there and you will be the envy of all the other growers.

Not only that but other growers will start coming to you for advice on how to deal with problems. They may even ask you to teach them how to grow using your system. Hell, I have done that very thing. I found a master grower and picked his brain for everything he is worth. You know what the end result was? I became a master grower too!

Don't reinvent the wheel. Just make it a little better!

Sometimes real live natural disasters happen such as fire, drought, earthquakes and storms. You should definitely have a plan for each and every one of these types of natural disasters. In some ways they are the easiest ones to plan for because there are clear cut procedures to follow when natural disasters strike.

Fire can be a real problem whether you are growing in the country or growing in town. If you are in town you basically have to leave it up to the fire department. If you are growing in the country you should try and create a fire line in order to protect your crops. If you have to evacuate you will be really glad that your system is automated watering. If the fire doesn't get you at least you'll have something to come back too. That is really all you can do.

Drought has been on everyone's mind recently. If you live in an area that is experiencing drought or low rainfall you need to store water. The best way to store water is during the rainy season. You need to use a catchment system and store as much as you think you will need for the season. Use the internet to get some sort of idea of how much you will probably use. I would tell you except each grow scene is different. Different size, different climate, different plant count, different media.... the list goes on and on. I can tell you that if you are growing a lot of weed you will need a lot of water. 100,000 gallons of water is not as much as you think.

Employees are disasters waiting to happen and you need to create a system so that you can deal with them successfully. You'll want criteria for hiring, and a checklist for giving them directions.

When you give your employees directions you need to be able to give the directions in a clear manner that is so easy a novice could understand them. I am being very serious. Your directions need to be broken down into steps. Don't skip steps! If you do so will they and you'll have only yourself to blame. You can't assume that they will be able to make intuitive leaps.

After you give them their instructions make them repeat the instructions back to you. You are going to freak out at how much is missed. Either they weren't paying attention or you suck at communication. It is probably a combo. Nobody is as good as they think they are at communicating.

Hopefully you will be able to get them to follow your instructions. I once had an employee who would not follow instructions. I would tell him what to do and show him exactly how I wanted him to do it. Then I would say "Okay your turn, let me see you do it". That fucker would always do it his own way even when I was standing right there! If heaven forbid you end up with one of these people replace them as soon as possible because they will ruin your business. Because, hey, they know what they are doing. Wrong, wrong, wrong!

The best way I have found to get workers to follow instructions is to create a step by step checklist. This can be somewhat of a pain in the ass but when it is done you are really sitting pretty. Why? Because now you can replace worker A with worker B if they don't follow instructions. And you should make it abundantly clear to your workers that with the easy to follow instructions anyone can do this job and that they are replaceable. It sucks. It's harsh. But that's business & real life.

When you first start creating your instructions you will have to imagine that you are doing the job yourself. You will probably miss steps but over time you will be able to refine your instructions to such a degree that they are essentially perfect. This will probably take a season or two but is well worth the effort.

Sometimes when you give your employees instructions they are just not going to understand what you are saying. This is your fault, not theirs. It is your job to be able to communicate with them in a manner that they understand. Sometimes this means you will have to tell them how to do the job a second time and you'll have to tell them in a different manner. You can do it!

You want a worker that follows instruction and nothing more! You don't want someone that starts "thinking" and decides to improve upon your system without consulting you first. Sometimes they have a valid point and their suggestion has merit. Often it does not because they are only focusing on one aspect of the garden whereas your instructions are designed for the benefit of the whole garden. That one change that they are trying to make may have catastrophic consequences for the rest of the garden.

You need to FEAR THE MOTIVATED IDIOT! The motivated idiot will ruin you and your life. The sad part is they were just trying to help. They just wanted to make it better. I have obviously been a victim of a motivated idiot. Often times their "improvement" has cost me thousands of dollars and hours of work. They have no idea that they are causing all sorts of future problems. You need to avoid these people like the plague.

An example of one of his improvements was that there was low water pressure in the garden in a certain spot. He decided to turn off a valve to increase the pressure over there and never turned it back on. The result? The other garden didn't get watered for 3 days! This really fucked up the plants and they never recovered.

His response? "I was only trying to help!" After that I implemented a strict "don't try to improve anything without talking to me first!" policy. I have kept to that policy and with it in place I have been able to minimize the negative consequences of the dreaded MOTIVATED IDIOT!

Your best recourse is to figure out who is a motivated idiot and get rid of them. If you can't get rid of them then you will need to reign them in with the "don't fuck with shit" policy and keep on them about it. Sorry.

Let's move on shall we?

Varmints. There are three varmints that you need to know about. They are rodents, deer, and bears.

Rats, mice, squirrels, gophers, and chipmonks are all rodents. They can and do cause damage to your garden. Here is a quick list of the damage that they can cause. They will eat your plants, eat into your water line, damage your plant roots and debranch your plants. You need to use two methods to stop these rodents from ruining your season.

The two best methods for stopping them in their tracks is to use rat traps and to place a barrier between your plant roots and the gopher.

You should never ever use poison. This only leads to massive problems. You never know what animal is going to ingest the poison. The poison is delivered in a yummy package so your dog or your friend's dog might eat it. Heaven forbid a child gets a hold of it. I don't even want to think about it. Well, it doesn't stop there. Let's imagine that the rodents do eat it and crawl off to die. There they are dead and full of poison, some predator will come along and eat that yummy dead rodent. That predator may be your dog, a skunk, a fox, an owl or…. The point is the poison doesn't just kill the rodents the poison kills other animals as well. Using poison is a great way to get the environmental agencies up your ass. So I suggest not using poison. Besides, trapping is just as effective.

The best type of bait to use in a rat trap is something that can be wedged onto the trigger. This way the rodent will have to fight to pull it off and trigger the trap. I like peanuts with the shell still on because you can wedge the shell on nice and tight.

You will also want to wire the trap to something permanent like a tree or a stake in the ground. Anything will work really. Why anchor? Let me tell you a little story. One time I was gardening in the woods back in the day. I had some nice new traps out, baited and set. I came back 3 days later and half my traps were gone! The other half were still loaded. I couldn't for the life of me figure out why they were gone. Did someone come into the garden and steal half my traps? No way! So I went looking for them around the perimeter of the garden. What I found really freaked me out.

I found one trap with just a rat head left in it and the trap was jammed up against the brush. My immediate reaction was "Holy fuck some sick fucking kids have found my garden and are doing some scary sick rituals here!" Then I thought about it for a minute and came up with more probable scenario. Maybe the trap caught a rat and then a skunk grabbed the carcass, still attached to the trap, and drug it off into the brush to enjoy a free meal.

Turns out this is exactly what happened! Boy was I relieved! I didn't have to deal with any crazy worshippers in the middle of the woods!

This is why you wire your traps to an object. It prevents predators from dragging the traps away.

If you are diligent in the beginning of the season with your trapping you will have cleared the area of rodents who walk on land. Even after you have eradicated the rodents you should keep the traps set, because new rodents show up when you least expect it.

To stop gophers all you need to do is place a barrier between your soil and the native soil. You can use small hole chicken wire, gopher cages, hardware cloth or Smart Pots. For some reason gophers don't really burrow through Smart Pot Fabric.

Deer are fairly easy to deal with. Just build a sturdy fence that is high enough that they can't jump over. Six feet is the usual proscribed height. If you don't protect your plants from deer they will eat your garden down to nub in no time flat.

Bear are somewhat easy to deal with. First of all, you can't stop them. They are going to do what they want. You could get an electric fence. That has been known to work. Sometimes it just pisses them off. If you chose an electric fence they do have solar ones that are supposed to be effective.

Bears are not interested in your plants. They are interested in food so your best defense is to avoid using products that will attract the bears. Things that have been known to attract bears are: molasses, bone meal, blood meal, fish emulsion, bukashi, shrimp meal. Basically anything that can be considered a food source for a bear. If they smell something yummy in your garden, or even beyond your garden, they will walk right through your fence to get what they want. It is best to not tempt them. Can you imagine what a bear could do to your garden if it smelled something yummy in the soil? I don't even want to think about. But I can say this: I have never had a bear kill my plants! Of course I have had them destroy a barrel of molasses. But no plants!

Pests can be a real problem and they are really beyond the scope of this book. The best thing that you can do when it comes to pests is to use preventative care and to kill them before they breed. Spray your plants regularly with kelp while they are growing and this will go a long way in preventing the pests from getting established. You should also spray once a week with a non toxic preventative pesticide while they are in vegetative state. Using this method will do wonders.

24 STAGING/TIME LINE/THE PLAN

The plan. What you need is a plan. I mean a real fucking plan that includes all the nuts and bolts. Your plan should include a schedule, when to start, when to finish and how to get there.

Regardless if you want to light dep or do long season you need a plan. Not only do you need a plan your plan should be written down. Many growers out there don't have a written plan and a lot of them do well. But a lot of them don't do well. If you take the time to develop a plan you will be able to determine your schedule for months to come and you will also see if what you are trying to pull off is possible.

In fact when you make your plan you might notice that you are actually underachieving. That is the beauty of a well thought out plan. The plan lets you schedule in the amount you are comfortable with and allows you to see if you are slacking or trying to do more than is possible.

Your plan will cover a lot of aspects of the growing season and if you are trying to pull off multiple harvests you are going to be having many things going on simultaneously. The only way to efficiently and realistically keep track of all this stuff is to have a plan.

The great news about making a plan is you only have to do it once in the beginning of the year. If you nail the plan and pull off what you wanted you can use the same plan again next year. However, if you were unable to make the plan work this season, then next season you can revise it and update it. This will make you a better grower next season and in the years to come.

The first thing you need to determine in your plan is how many harvests do you want to do this upcoming season? Once you have determined exactly how many harvests you want to pull off you will be able to calculate how many plants you will need, how much work you are going to have to do, when to start cuttings, when to transplant, and when to harvest. Of course a lot more will go into it than this, but you get the idea.

Something to consider is this: the more harvests that you want to pull in one season the more money you will have to spend up front. Assuming everything is in place such as infrastructure, soil and frames you will still need to spend money on either buying clones or making them. You will need to buy fertilizers and all sorts of little shit. No matter how well you plan you will always need to make a run to the store for something at least once a week. Stuff breaks, you run out of something, or as you go along you see ways to improve upon what you built in the first place. Hence the visits to the store.

Make sure that you set aside some money to deal with these early and late season problems because they will happen.

Once you have determined how many runs you want to pull off you need to establish a timeline. To establish a timeline you will need to create a work calendar. On this calendar you will have your start times and harvest times. Seems pretty simple and for the most part it is. The complex part is how many different things that you will have to be doing day in and day out. If you don't write it down on a calendar there is no way you will be able to keep track of everything that needs to get done, and done on time.

Time is the real problem here. If you are trying to pull off two or more harvests in a year then you need to make the basic assumption that time is working against you. Not only is it working against you but you are already behind schedule. This is the mindset that you must have to really kick ass.

You can't afford to be lackadaisical with what needs to get done because every day that you put something off is a week that it puts you behind. If you slack just a little bit before you know it the season is over and you will have only accomplished a fraction of your goals. So buck up, cowboy, and get your nose to the grindstone.

Growing weed, contrary to popular belief, is hard work. I mean hard work in the true sense of the word. You are a farmer. This means you need to haul soil around, move plants, transplant, water, prune, feed your plants, protect your plants from predators and all sorts of other shit.

I am not saying this to scare you, I am just telling you the truth you already know. Growing weed ain't for the lazy people. Not if you want to really succeed at it.

To really be able to fill in your calendar you need to schedule in your harvests dates. For the ease of explanation let's assume that you are going to try to pull off three harvests. This is always where you start. You want to start with your last harvest NOT the first one. There is a simple reason for this. Once you know when your end date is for your 3rd run you can calculate backwards in time when you need to transplant for the 3rd run. This also means you know when you need to harvest the 2nd run in order to be able to start the 3rd run. This also means that you will know when you need to transplant your 2nd run and when you need to harvest your 1st run. But wait- there's more. This also means that you will know when you need to transplant your 1st run into the dep. Now you see why you need to not only figure out how many runs you want to do but also when you want to harvest your last run.

With your final harvest date chosen you can set some of the major milestone markers on your calendar. Now you need to fill in the other major milestones, but you will need some information first…

If you are buying clones make sure that you place your order far out in advance. Also, please follow up on the status of your clone order. This is not something that you want to overlook because if your clones aren't ready on time you are in big trouble!

If you are taking your own clones you need to be able to figure out how long it takes from cutting a clone to a fully rooted clone. The simple answer is anywhere from 10 to 21 days. I have had clones root in 10 days and I have had clones root in 21 days. A lot of this depends on the technique you use and the plant variety that you use.

There are a lot of great cloning techniques out there. You need to do some serious research unless you already have a good technique. In my opinion a good technique needs to have the following qualities: repeatable, fast, easy, and low maintenance.

I know that sounds like a lot to ask but, trust me, it is not. I have seen at least 10 different cloning techniques fulfill all of those criteria. Granted, I have been around awhile. Pretty much all of the techniques out there are very similar. So find one that works for you

and master it. Don't try to create shortcuts. Just repeat what you learned and you will probably be good to go.

Varieties do play a big role in how long a cutting will take to root. Most green weed will root in 10 to 14 days. OG's on the other hand can be exceptionally hard to root. If you are making your own clones and haven't mastered how to clone OG you may want to stick to an easier variety to clone until you get more experience with the OG. If you are depending on the clones that you are making and they don't root you are fucked. You should grow and clone something you know that you can easily get to root. Try some Sour Diesel instead. That is a fairly easy variety to root and everybody loves Sour D!!

The point here is it takes 10 to 21 days to root a cutting. I always assume that it will take 21 days when I schedule my calendar out. Remember our assumption that time is against you and it is later than you think.

If a cutting takes 21 days to root how long does it take a rooted clone to get to transplant size? That is a great question. Depending on the variety, light intensity, pot size, and vigor of the plant it will take approximately 5 weeks to get your rooted clone to transplant size. Transplant size is approximately 18 inches tall and 12 inches wide.

Of course, there are certain assumptions that I am making. Here are my assumptions: healthy clone, ample light, 1 gallon pot, adequate feeding, and a good watering schedule. When you transplant your clone I am assuming that the clone has a decent root system. Nothing crazily over developed and nothing under developed. The assumption is that you will actually see a couple of roots sticking out of the media.

You should be transplanting into a 1 gallon pot. This allows your clone to freely grow some good roots without worrying about getting root bound. A 1 gallon pot is ideal in my opinion versus a 4 inch pot because you won't have to transplant from the 4 inch to a 1 gallon. You should just save yourself some work and plant directly into the 1 gallon pot. The 1 gallon pot will give your plant enough soil to grow into a good size plant which is 18 inches tall and 12 inches wide.

Obviously your plants will need several hours of light a day to do this and they must never experience more than 6 hours of uninterrupted darkness. This will keep them in a nice vegetative state. Additionally, they will also need at least 6 hours of high intensity light daily to be able to grow at a rate that will get them to size in 5 weeks. You need to figure out how your plants are going to be able to get that 6 hours or more of high intensity light. You can grow them indoors or you can grow them in a greenhouse with some lights. Whatever method you choose is okay as long as you get it done.

During the 5 week period of growth make sure to feed your plants and water them appropriately. If you are really on it you can spray them once a day with kelp. Spraying your plants really does increase the growth rate. I have seen a side by side experiment and the difference after 21 days was shocking. The side that was being sprayed daily was on average 5 inches taller!

So here we are. We took the cuttings and they took 3 weeks to root. Then we transplanted the clone into a 1 gallon pot and let it grow under high intensity light for five weeks. We now have a plant that is 18 inches tall and 12 inches wide and ready to transplant into its final location.

That was a total of 8 weeks from cutting to transplant ready. Basically it took two months to get your plants where they needed to be. Did you think it would take that long? Or did you think it would take longer? Either way, here we are.

With the knowledge that is going to take two months to get your plants ready to transplant and an additional week for them to get established once transplanted you can now fill in the rest of the major mile markers for each run. At this point it should be pretty easy to do. If you want a shortcut you can visit my website and I'll give you a free copy of my Light Dep Harvest Calendar. The only caveat is the calendar was designed with 8 weeker strains in mind.

You can grab your copy of the calendar at humboldtlightdep.com/resources

The important thing to remember with these assumptions is plant density. I am assuming that you will be planting plants approximately 18 to 24 inches apart when you plant them in the light dep. This will help you to figure out exactly how many starts you are going to need to get through each run.

After you have calculated how many plants you are going to need for each run you will need to make sure that you have enough space to grow your plants up to size in the 1 gallon pots. If we are shooting for each 1 gallon pot to take up 1 foot in diameter when it's ready for transplanting then that means you can only fit 100 plants in a 10 foot by 10 foot space. I know- that's a lot of space for such a small amount of plants.

But it is very important to give your plants the space they need to grow so that they can actually achieve the size that you are going to need.

Of course when you first transplant them into the 1 gallon pot you can pack them in super tight. As they grow it is very important to start spacing them out so that they can get the light that they need. When you create the proper staging/growing area for your plant requirements you will make your life a lot easier by having a location that will be used again and again.

This is a very important aspect of growing or building your plants to size that you need to consider and account for. Because if your plants can't get to the size you need them, when you need them, then you are not going to achieve the goals you have set for yourself. You may need to build a temporary greenhouse or rent a room to get your plants to size.

Now you literally have all the key information to set yourself up for major success for the 1st run. By working backward you know when you need to take your cuttings. You know how many you need and how long to grow them before transplanting.

After creating your calendar you will also know when you need to do all those steps for the 2nd and 3rd run! I hope you see why it is so important that you actually write this down on a calendar- because there really is a lot to keep track of and it would be so easy to forget just one step.

Can you imagine if you forgot to take your cuttings on time and were two weeks late? Can you see how that would really put a massive wrench in your plans? I have done exactly that in the past. That is why I use a calendar for scheduling. I know what works and when to do it. I don't need to worry or think about it too much because my trusty external hard drive (the calendar) is right there reminding me what to do at the appropriate time!

If you don't like the idea of running small plants as I suggested all you need to do is add a week or two to the five weeks of vegetative growth and your plants will get a lot bigger. Of course if you grow your plants much longer than five weeks in a 1 gallon pot your plants will more than likely get root bound. This means if you want them a bit bigger, you would be better off using a 2 gallon pot instead of a 1 gallon pot. This also means that you will need more area to grow your plants to the size that you want them. None of this is a problem as long as you account for it in your plan.

So get off your butt, bust out a calendar and get to planning today before it gets too late. Remember- it's later than you think.

ABOUT THE AUTHOR

James Defenbaugh is a good ol' Humboldt County boy. He lives smack dab in the middle of California's Emerald Triangle. With a lifetime spent in working out in the hills and a Bachelor of Science in Environmental Resources Engineering James' mission is to provide knowledge & products to help growers take their gardens to the next level. In 2015 James founded Humboldt Light Dep Company to develop *affordable* light dep greenhouses & retrofit kits. You can keep up with his latest projects at humboldtlightdep.com

Made in the USA
San Bernardino, CA
29 June 2019